Great
Relief

Great Relief

Nine Sacred Secrets Your Body Wants You
To Know About Freedom, Love, Trust,
And the Core Wound of Your Life

By Saniel Bonder

Mt. Tam Empowerments

Published by Mt. Tam Empowerments, Inc.

Cover design and interior layout by Susan MacLean
Back cover photo by Al Porter

Orders and information: Ma-Tam Temple of Being
www.wakingdown.org, greatrelief@earthlink.net
toll-free (U.S.) 888-741-5000

ISBN 0-9753532-1-7

CONTENTS

For Linda,
who always knew

FOREWORD
Body Language

On the day after Christmas in 1999, I started writing a book on the deeper mysteries of life using, if possible, nothing but "body language" – the simplest possible words for our most primal feelings and realities.

Great Relief is the result of that effort. I hope it speaks to you. I hope it speaks to you even if you like books written in sophisticated psychological, scientific, philosophical, or spiritual language.

But I especially hope it speaks to you if you don't like such books, even don't know what such a book would be like, but find something appealing here.

When I finally finished the book early this month, a little over four years after starting it, I felt humbled and silent, as well as grateful.

I offer it both into your hands and at your feet; for your eyes or ears to take into your heart; and thence to your whole body and your whole being.

Saying all that, now that I've written it and put it before you, I feel as if my heart is grinning wide. I hope you'll feel the same way while you read or listen and when you've finished it, too.

So many people have helped me bring this book into being that I can't possibly name you all here. To each and all, many thanks.

Saniel Bonder
At the feet of Mt. Tamalpais
San Rafael, California
April 2004

SECRET #1

Most Every Body Feels Like Something Is Fundamentally Wrong, Missing, or Unclear at the Core of Life Most of the Time

Is something wrong?

What prompted you to pick up a book with this title or subtitle?

Do you have a feeling that something is missing in your spirit, your soul, your life? Something's not quite right? Unclear? Not complete? Not fulfilling enough? Nowhere near satisfying?

Do you feel like you don't fit in your own body, or in this world at all? Even if you have the trappings of success and fulfillment – in career, family, religious faith, spiritual experience, money, possessions, friendships, favorite things to do and places to go – do you feel trapped among the trappings? Even trapped by them? Is something still missing?

Or is a lot missing? Do you feel severe hopelessness, worthlessness, desolation? Are you just about at wits' end, or maybe even past it? Have you sometimes wondered why you even bother to go on living?

Either way, or at any place on the spectrum between "something's not right here" and "everything's dreadful here," I suggest the essence of what you are suffering is not going to be touched by any changes you can make in your activities, your relationships, your health, your wealth, your situation – even any changes you can make in your mind or your feelings and assumptions about life. It's deeper and more central than all that. It's *fundamental*.

I also suggest that this fundamental "something wrong-ness" is not bad. It is not wrong. You are not wrong for feeling it. It's not an indication of your personal or spiritual unworthiness, irresponsibility, or laziness. It's not a consequence of your having failed to fulfill the divine commandments of any prophet or religion. It's not proof of your jinxed destiny or bad karma.

The core wound. Rather, that most essential distress is what I call "the core wound." The core wound is not evidence of a degraded human estate. On the contrary, I hold it to be an evolutionary hallmark of our humanness. The more sensitive you become to and *as* this core wound, the more you advance in human evolution.

Thus, the root of our suffering, this core wound, is not evil, and it's not sin. It constitutes the marrow of our true dignity as human beings – even when we appear to have no dignity at all. But it *is* painful. It's often excruciating, and sometimes, at last, impossible to endure.

Matt and his suicide. One story of how the core wound can become too much to bear involves the self-inflicted death of a talented, sensitive, and ambitious young man whom we'll call Matt.

I never met Matt. In the spring of 1998, I met and spoke just once with his family. Two weeks before, Matt had jumped to his death off the Golden Gate Bridge in San Francisco.

The young woman who was Matt's girlfriend, Marie, had been aware of my spiritual work for some time. Shortly after Matt's death she commented to his mother that Matt had not been able, while alive here, to heal his core wound. (I'll be saying a lot more later about what exactly we can and can't heal. Actually, it's not the core wound itself that can be healed, but rather our chronic, more or less unconscious relationship to it.)

Marie's comments prompted his mother and sister to ask if I could come help them in their shock and grief. I tried my best, knowing they had been dealt a grievous blow they can never fully recover from in this lifetime.

Of course, many other insights might be offered about what makes a man take his own life. Whatever we may know or think about why one would do it, those who survive a loved one's suicide are left to stare into a chasm of unspeakable darkness, bewilderment – and horror.

Yet, for me at least, what Matt's grieving lover said about him did bear a certain likely truth. The pain and pressure of the core wound had perhaps become too great for him to endure.

Whatever anyone else might have done in his predicament, Matt felt he had to take himself out of this life. He sensed and already felt terrible about how much pain he would be causing his loved ones. He apologized for this in his final letter to them. But he had to do it.

In killing himself, did Matt commit an unforgivable sin, even an ultimate one? Did he cast his soul into a hell of condemnation, of certain, even perpetual dis-grace?

I don't think so.

His extreme action had and continues to have consequences – obviously for those who survive him, and I expect for his own soul as well. If that's the case, he, like everyone he left behind here, will have to deal with those consequences.

But is this about damnation? Again, I don't think so.

You're welcome to disagree with me about this. At last none of us can grasp all the consequences of others' actions, or even our own. Nor can we do more than speculate on what may or may not happen after anyone's bodily life here ends.

We probably can agree on one thing, however. Regardless of their reactions to it and the consequences of those reactions, for

some people the pain of being alive here on Earth is extreme. That
pain wrecks their entire lives.

For many others, that pain, while not so extreme, still
disturbs, aggravates, and disorients them most if not all the time.
As a result, they never, ever know there may be an alternative way
to be here.

Freedom, love, and trust in the world of living paradox.
When we get to the root of that pain and distress, we find what
I call the core wound. Or, to say it more directly, when *you* get
to that root of pain and distress in yourself, you find *your*
core wound.

In Secrets #1 through #7, we'll investigate some of the ways
we register the impact and reality of the core wound – from a
bodily perspective that is simple yet profound. In Secret #8 I'll
venture a definition of that core wound. Then in Secret #9 I'll
tell you the essential thing I've learned about how we can heal
our relationship to this primal reality of our lives and make it
increasingly conscious. Throughout the book, I'll offer perspectives
and true stories that can allow us to deepen our understanding of
the core wound and thus open ourselves to greater relief.

The more sensitized you become to this wound at the root
of life and awareness, the more relief and freedom you will feel.
But you won't experience relief *from* that core wound. The series of
insights, openings, and recognitions you may go through will help
you accept the core wound as a foundational reality of your life.
Strangely, you'll begin to feel it's not something you suffer that is
happening to you. You'll begin to feel the core wound is what you
are *being*.

If that sounds like a contradiction, welcome to the world of
living paradox! In this realm of paradox, what we used to assume
were mutually exclusive opposites now appear to coincide. In this
case, those opposites are (a) greater sensitivity to the pain and
pressure of this wound I'm describing and (b) greater relief and

freedom, presumably from the very same pain! (Maybe we should label the greater relief and freedom "(z)," since it appears to be the total opposite of (a).)

Similarly, the more relief and freedom you feel at the heart of your existence, the more love you will be able to give and receive, and the more you will feel you are living *in and as love,* even in the midst of your own and others' pain.

And, somehow all the more central to our wellness of being, the more you do live in such freedom and in and as such love, the more you will discover you are also abiding in *trust* of life itself. You will find a quality of trust you have never known before. Not in religious belief or faith, not in spiritual experience or surrender, not in any human or natural confidence in yourself, others, or the world.

Freedom. Love. Trust. These develop gradually. For some, they may become the unshakable foundations of a new kind of life. That new life has its own challenges. After living it awhile you forget the sufferings of unconscious coping with the core wound that you experienced for so long. The world of living paradox appears designed to provide tests, trials, delights and agonies sufficient to temper and grow us in our enjoyment of great relief.

But for everyone who benefits from even one of these secrets to any degree, there will be at least some small liberation. There will be a deeper feeling of the indescribable mystery of just being alive. There will be a touch of joy, a glimpse of something special, something even holy and divine, right here in your own life, your own body. That's why I call these secrets "sacred." It may sound sacrilegious to your mind or soul to think of these bodily intimations of freedom, love, and trust as holy things. But your heart and body may well *feel* that way about them, nonetheless.

The good medicine of "taking a breath." I'll say more about this world of living paradox in discussing Secret #2 and later on in the book.

A few moments ago we were peering into the chasm of suicide and death.

Just now I've been suggesting that the great relief we can find results from becoming *more* sensitive to the essential pain at the core of our lives, not less.

We've jumped right in to some challenging things to look at and feel together.

Let's take a breath.

Did you actually take that breath? Go ahead. Put the book down and really take a deep inhalation and exhalation before you pick it up again.

Before we go on, let me propose a more complete approach to "taking a breath" that allows you to stop and integrate yourself with everything you may be feeling and thinking as you read or listen. This is a good way to complete a current of investigation, clearing the air of our whole being and readying ourselves to go further.

I'll recommend exercises and journaling ideas for each of this book's nine secrets. Even just to read through these recommendations might be of benefit to you. If you aren't inclined to do any of them, that's totally fine. They're not necessary unless you find them to be! Yet if you don't try them, you won't know how helpful they might have been. So I urge you to give each of them a whirl and see for yourself.

Exercise for Secret #1: "Take a breath, relax, and feel into this first secret." Do this in a situation where you can relax and not have to respond to other stimuli. If you're listening to this book on tape or CD while driving a car, of course you want to remain alert to where you are and what you're doing.

Here's the simple practice:

- Take a deep inhalation
- Perhaps hold that breath for a brief time
- Then let that breath out, as if your whole body were a lung and you were exhaling out of every pore
- Now relax as deeply as you can, as if your body were melting into the chair or seat you're sitting on, or into the bed or couch if you are lying down
- Somewhere in the midst of that whole cycle of breathing, stretch and then tense, shake, or shudder your whole body, every muscle you can
- Then release all the tightness and effort – that often aids the relaxation
- Repeat the whole exercise, or any part of it, as often as you like

If you are tense to start with, you may find relaxing difficult. That's okay. There's no success or failure here. No one's judging your effort. *This is not a test.*

You may be disappointed if you find it difficult to relax much. In that case, the further recommendation I'm going to be making throughout this book is simple:

Just feel the disappointment.

Feel the tension – and feel the difficulty you're having in letting go of it, or in relaxing through and beyond it.

Should it arise yet again, feel the further disappointment that comes up for you because it appears you can't do something as simple as relaxing. "And *now* I'm having a hard time even feeling my disappointment!"

Every now and again, as we go through these secrets, I'll say, "Take a breath." What I'll be meaning is just this exercise I've outlined.

Let's try it again.

Take a breath.

You don't have to wait for me to make the suggestion. Also, if you have other practices you already know that will help you relax more fully, do them whenever you like. Just try not to get all tensed up about doing things right, stressfully performing exercises to relax!

I'm assuming, then, that at the moment you're relaxing as deeply as you can.

Relaxation and feeling are linked. The quality of feeling I'm talking about here is not identical to any particular emotion or any specific emotional reaction. It's a kind of tone, temper, or mood of your whole being. Once you start to get in touch with this quality of whole-being, whole-body feeling, you will have more access to particular *feelings* that come up in you in response to the events of life.

Now, having done an exercise of breathing and relaxing as much as possible into generalized whole-body feeling, see what particular feelings and thoughts may be coming up for you about the topic of this chapter.

The enormity – and the dignity – of our predicament. Let's look again at Secret #1:

"Most Every Body Feels Like Something Is Fundamentally Wrong, Missing, or Unclear at the Core of Life Most of the Time."

Do you feel that proposition is true?

I think many people would agree it is. Even many individuals who would say it is not true about *them* would agree that it's true of most every body they know.

I am not saying that most every body *thinks* something is fundamentally wrong, missing, or unclear in this way. I am saying most every body *feels* it. There's an underlying agitation in most humans that few of us, perhaps, would even admit. Even when we're saying all is right and well in our lives, or most everything, or at least the most fundamental things, most every body is still, underneath, registering this central, distressful something.

Before we rush in to fix that something, whatever we may call it, let's acknowledge the scope of this predicament, if I've characterized it at all accurately. Here we are who knows how many millennia down the road of human history and evolution, and still, somehow, most every human being alive feels like something in her or his life is fundamentally *off*.

Most of the six billion plus members of our species are reacting nearly all the time to the distress this fundamental lack, or feeling of off-ness, causes us. The argument could certainly be made that this is the single most defining feature of human life and culture.

That's the enormity of the situation.

We're not going to handle this problem any time soon. The UN is not going to come out with a great international program for it. Visitors from other planets, if they exist, are not going to miraculously transform our nervous systems and take care of it. No great Savior or Philosopher-King, nor any sublime, democratic Leadership Team, is going to slay this dragon and save the day, to be praised in song by every human heart until the end of time.

If you're a religious or spiritual person and your beliefs move you to assume, hope, and pray for that kind of miraculous intervention, let me just ask you to acknowledge that, for now at least, its immediate likelihood may not be great.

For better or worse, our beliefs – our religions, philosophies, psychologies, and self-help teachings – often fail to just let us feel the vexing reality of that core-level "something's-wrongness." They're vying for our allegiance and loudly urging us to do this or that about this central ill-at-ease-ness we feel. They all mean well. They were created or revealed by sincere, earnest, inspired people, some of them saints and god-like human beings. But it may just be that they fail to deal effectively with this central human issue.

Let's face it, we all – nearly all, anyway – to some degree want or need to be *right*. To have the security of owning the really truest truth. Myself included! Even this book on some levels can't help but contribute to all the cranky, irritating static in our systems about whose truth is really True.

So I don't think any conclusive divine intervention, proof of any one believable truth, or objectively verifiable saving of the total human day, is going to happen. Not any time soon, and, just maybe, never *ever*.

Because in all likelihood, we human beings are not even going to get close to agreeing about what the problem really is here. Much less on any single, absolute fact or action that is the be-all and end-all cure for it.

All of that further underlines the enormity of the situation.

The dignity comes in sitting back – perhaps taking a breath or two! – and acknowledging that this is our reality. This is how it is for nearly every human being on Earth. And this is how it is for *us*, personally.

Nearly every single one of us feels like something is fundamentally wrong, missing, or unclear right at the very heart of our existence.

Don't worry – I certainly do feel that each one of us can heal or outgrow our more or less unconscious relationship to that wound.

Remember, this is a living paradox. The great relief I'm offering comes not by trying to banish this core reality of our lives.

Instead, it comes by our acceptance of it by degrees, even so much that we *become* it.

I will tell you why that is, how you can achieve this great relief, and what it entails as we proceed. I'm not just going to leave you with the illness and no prognosis for the kind of wellness that is really possible.

The first step in any healing, however – even one like this that's not exactly a "cure" – is acknowledging that something is wrong. Like people trying to get clean and sober in 12-step programs that deal with addictions, our first great step toward health is admitting to ourselves and then to the world that we are ill.

For those of you who are reading the book, to give you a little more breathing space, we are starting each exercise, journaling suggestion, and chapter conclusion on its own page. So, when you're ready for another exercise, please turn to page 12.

Another exercise for Secret #1: Try confessing it aloud to yourself in a mirror, and then to someone you know well and trust.

- Look at yourself in the mirror, gazing directly into your own eyes
- Say to yourself, and to the universe and all beings, including any God or Goddess you may worship or believe in, "My name is _____ and I feel like something is fundamentally wrong, missing, or unclear at the core of my life most if not all of the time"
- If you feel adventurous, ask a friend or loved one, someone you know well and trust, to sit with you
- Look them in the eye and tell them the same exact thing you just told yourself

Having made this admission, now just sit or stand there and feel how it feels to have done so.

If you tried this with a friend or loved one, let him or her make the same admission to you. And afterward the two of you can talk about how you each feel, how you reacted, what this exercise brought up in you.

My bet is, if you've done either or both forms of the exercise, right now you may feel both a sigh of relief and a strange exhilaration in your body.

Your emotions and thoughts may be quite turbulent. But I bet your body, at a sense-feeling level, finds the whole event enlivening and positively provocative.

The reason this is where I place my bet is because of what I've observed over many years of working with people around these issues. I've noticed that people start to come alive in a whole new way as soon as they can make this kind of sincere confession to themselves and others.

That may seem weird – feeling better as soon as you can say aloud, even just to yourself, how fundamentally weird or bad you feel at the core of your life. Again, welcome to that world of living paradox.

This is a real confession. There is something spontaneously sacred about it. "'Fessing up" this way feels almost holy. It allows primal feelings that we've held down, stifled, and suppressed, perhaps even all our lives, to come way up and out. We dare to become known to ourselves and others by the authentic, previously hidden reality that we've spoken out loud at last.

That act sets us human beings freer in our real bodily lives than we've ever been before. It speaks a truth of the body that the mind or soul may not feel very comfortable acknowledging. The body, however, tends to delight in this truth. The body has unthinkingly felt all along that *this is how life really is.*

That's why just getting Secret #1 a little bit can itself depressurize your whole life in a wonderful way. You'll see as we go along that every one of these secrets holds that kind of potential – for you and other people. When deeply felt into, every one of these bodily secrets of freedom, love, and trust can grant some degree of great relief. All by itself! Taken together, this whole book of them can make life much more bearable and sane, even in the midst of crises and hard times.

What I mean when I speak of "the body." Let's back up just a little. When I speak of "the body" or "your body," and especially when I make distinctions, as just above, between "the body" and "the mind or soul," I am doing so with considerable awareness of many currents of thought, from ancient, medieval, and modern sources, about the relationship between spirit and matter and the nature of mind, psyche, and/or soul.

Some traditional wisdom suggests that human beings have several different "bodies," which surround one another like the layers of an onion, except that the subtler bodies interpenetrate, successively, each of the grosser ones. They speak of these bodies as "sheaths." Some suggest there are five basic sheaths in our total constitution; others, more; a few, fewer. Traditional Hindu yoga from India, for instance, identifies a physical sheath, an energetic one, two different sheaths comprising the more outward and inward, or coarser and more refined, dimensions of mind and psyche, and one that is the core of both identity and attention. The subtler sheaths permeate the grosser ones. And so on.

I could get into that kind of hair-splitting or onion-peeling, but it would introduce unnecessary complications in this book. Here it should be enough to say that when I distinguish "the body" from "the mind or soul," I am pointing not just to an inert physical sheath or portion of our being, a dumb chunk of merely sensate matter. I am pointing, rather, to the vibrant, vital, and in its own way quite intelligent, material part of our being, which also includes a variety of cell-based qualities of mind and psyche.

I'm not trying to conform what I say to any previous discussion or theory about human nature, such as formal psychological theories about the subconscious and unconscious minds. Rather, I am expressing what my own adventures in self-transformation and my observations of others suggest to me. It appears to me that most of us are suffering a more or less unwitting split between our relatively self-aware ego-sense, mind, psyche, and/or soul, and our relatively un-self-aware material, bodily being, whose intelligence seems to be suppressed, stifled, and unexpressed in our daily living.

On one plane, this whole book is attempting to give voice to that unexpressed body-intelligence and to integrate it with all the rest of who and what we are. That's what these secrets are all about!

Journaling on Secret #1. You might now record in a journal whatever feelings, thoughts, reactions, and responses you wish, including anything that's come up about the whole process of confessing how you fundamentally feel in the ways I've suggested.

Three general types of great relief. My wife Linda Groves-Bonder (who sings professionally under her birth name Linda Groves) came up with a beautiful insight into the qualities of great relief that are possible for three general types of readers of or listeners to this book. I've taken her ideas and worked them into the presentation that follows here. Linda and our colleagues and I look forward to helping others find where they fit in this general description and access the kinds of relief or release they really desire.

Great Relief for the Everyday Hero or Heroine. The first is any person who wants ease from some of the pressures of living and wants to understand why life is the way it is. By "everyday" I don't mean typical, average, humdrum, mediocre, or unremarkable. But, by "hero" or "heroine" I don't mean outstanding, amazing people living dramatic and world-shaking lives, either.

I am talking about so many of us who are embodying our values and refining our characters in the midst of all kinds of everyday circumstances that test and temper us. If you scratch the surface of most people's lives even a little bit, you will find currents of courage, compassion, and wisdom, of intelligence, discipline, humor, and so many other virtues. That's the kind of everyday hero or heroine we're talking about.

One of the primary characteristics of these people in this conversation is that – in contrast to the two other categories of people we're speaking about, as you will see below – they don't *principally* define themselves in religious or spiritual terms.

What are some of the character traits of an everyday heroine? Though she may believe in God – most people do –

she's not striving urgently for religious salvation. She's probably not active in any organized religion, even if she's a member of a congregation. She's also not seeking spiritual enlightenment. She doesn't need her version of great relief to make her religious or spiritual in some special way, any more than she knows she already is when just looking at a flower or holding her loved one's hand. Such a person is not self-consciously religious or spiritual.

This everyday person is simply living her life and finding it "too much" or "not enough." She may feel a void at the heart of life, an emptiness, a feeling of malaise or being ill at ease. She notices that the solutions to pain and distress advertised in the mass media and elsewhere do not deliver results, except at superficial levels. She finds herself yearning for a deeper comprehension of what's going on and why everything feels so intense, pressurized, debilitating or disorienting.

The kind of great relief such an everyday heroine can gain from this book and related communications is simple release from the most fundamental pressures of daily living in today's world. Through her contemplation of these secrets, she can discover a new lease on her life, a freedom from conflicting theories and opinions that, previously, she had struggled with but was not sure why. Her great relief can liberate her into living her life with more energy, serenity, and confidence.

How so? Because allowing these secrets to become her own wisdom will help her stop adding stressful reactions to certain harsh realities of life that she can't really change but which she previously was under the impression she could, or should. It will help her stop adding unnecessary pain to inevitable pain. It's as simple as that.

The same is true for the two other general types of potential beneficiaries of great relief. What differentiates them from the everyday hero or heroine and from each other is not how they come into the great relief that is possible for them, but rather certain forms that great relief can take due to their different dispositions and life needs.

Great Relief for the Religious Believer. The second type of person who can enjoy great relief is the religious believer, the man or woman of faith.

Please note that I am not saying that any religion is better or truer than any other. I am instead offering the benefit of this book's perspectives to any sincere religious person. Hateful, mean-spirited fundamentalists and "mine-is-the-only-real-God" fanatics won't be attracted to these teachings anyway.

Some of the people I'm pointing to here might object to being called "believers." They might say their faith is a much deeper thing than simple mental conviction. Their faith is a matter of the heart and whole being. Good! That's the kind of person I am talking about here, one whose whole human identity springs from a deep, faith-full life of religious awareness and observance.

Even so, many such religious people today find irresolvable conflicts between the faith they love and what appears to be contrary evidence in the real world of living with family, friends, and all other humans. The apparently endless succession of news stories about religious ministers and spiritual counselors exploiting and abusing others, even children; the seeming insensitivity of many theological and spiritual leaders to the real-life concerns and dilemmas of their congregants; the ways in which some religious leaderships appear to look the other way from the most distressing and difficult issues of our time; the violence with which fundamentalists and fanatics of differing faiths are willing to condemn and destroy human life – these and other contradictions torment many religious people who need to maintain both inquiring minds and compassionate hearts.

The kind of relief that such a person can enjoy by taking this book deeply to heart will grant him deliverance from a subtle but in many cases debilitating inner conflict. It may open him into a more mature, serene understanding of his faith, one that accommodates the "gray zones" of real life more easily without compromising his true integrity. This in turn will help him appreciate his personal religion all the more – even among all the other faiths in the world – and practice its precepts with more gratitude, energy, happiness, insight, and compassion.

These releases and openings won't tend to resolve the large social and moral issues surrounding religion in the world today. They might therefore move the serious believer who benefits from them into taking more active personal responsibility. They might liberate him into doing things about what disturbs him in his own life and in the larger society that he wouldn't have dared before. Or they might just give him breathing space and a greater core of strength to make a difference simply by practicing his treasured religious precepts in a quiet way in the local universe of his daily life and personal relationships.

Great Relief for the Spiritual Practitioner. The third type of person who may benefit from this book is an active – perhaps frustrated – spiritual practitioner or seeker. Spiritual practitioners are not necessarily religious believers in any particular God or faith. But they are active applicants of methods and techniques, ranging from meditation to rituals to therapeutic regimens, that they believe will help them become better, wiser, more compassionate people, and will someday allow them to become spiritually enlightened.

Many a spiritual practitioner hits a wall at some point in her journey where, like the religious believer, she feels conflicts between either the philosophies or the methods of her chosen practice and the realities that confront her in her daily life. She often can't find words to describe how these conflicts disturb her, but they certainly do. The interior pressures of these contradictions may exhaust her and make her incapable of fulfilling her chosen disciplines. In many cases this in turn can lead to extreme agitation, despair, resignation, or even cynicism.

The great relief that the spiritual practitioner taps into can have two general effects. If he is inclined to remain with the system, philosophy, and techniques he has already embraced, the secrets he accesses through this book can help him clarify his commitment. This allows him to refocus on his disciplines with greater wisdom, passion, and humor, all at once. Like the religious believer and the everyday, heroic person, such a practitioner will view life with an opened perspective that permits more mystery, more apparent contradiction, more depth and paradox.

If, in contrast, he is a severely frustrated or even burned out seeker, this book can reveal a whole new realm of understanding and exploration of life. That kind of seeker is ripe for "finding" what he has been so ardently looking for. He wants to end the search once and for all! He wants out of the whole life and the motivating anxiety that has made him seek so long and hard with, to now, such disappointing results. To him, the great relief he gravitates into may prove a gateway to marvels. It may uncover so much more of him and of life than he ever even hoped to find and grace him with unimagined appointments with destiny.

Some people may discover that they have elements of two or even all three of these kinds of person in themselves. The relief they find will be correspondingly rich, complex, and multidimensional. So be it! From time to time in the book I will refer to these three types of people and what changes they may discover. But you and I can know that the three types are not mutually exclusive, nor are their descriptions in any sense absolutely definitive.

We're much more paradoxical creatures than that!

At the end of the book, in the Afterword, "Where Can I Go from Here?," I'll tell you about sequels to *Great Relief* that I am planning to prepare soon. (I also mention them in the text and in footnotes.) Each of those books will also have relevance to one or more of these three general kinds of readers or listeners and their particular needs.

And, in the concluding paragraphs of each chapter, I'll indicate some of the possible qualities of relief that any of us can find by allowing that particular secret to deeply sink in. Taken together, these secrets can unburden us progressively and change our lives much for the better. And yet, as you'll see, each one also reveals another, perhaps deeper level of stress, confusion, or dilemma to be felt into and released in turn. Starting here with Secret #1.

Conclusion – the great relief we can find in Secret #1.
Let's now summarize the main points of this opening chapter.

This is our body's reality: It feels like something is fundamentally wrong, missing, or unclear right at the core of life most of the time.

Admitting that truth, painful and unsettling as it may be, is the first step on the road to fundamental rightness, completeness, and clarity – here at the heart-center of our bodies and our lives.

This single act frees up energy and attention we've had to devote to hiding and suppressing that terrible truth. And this liberation sometimes produces a huge rush, a movement to do other things differently too, to make things right, to achieve what we most desire. But it may not produce any such thing, either.

Whatever it brings forth in you is just right for you. Really! Whether you are an everyday hero, a religious believer, or a spiritual practitioner, or some combination of those, the encounter with this secret (and all the rest, too) is your own event. Its developments are not predictable according to others' experience.

All things considered, though, giving your body the opportunity to just 'fess up to how living actually is for you on these levels is very likely to be freeing. However you actually experience it, this admission certainly does unburden you. What it relieves you of might be in retrospect obvious: a sense that not only is there something wrong, missing, or unclear at the core of your life, but also that you shouldn't be feeling that way, and, therefore, that you are adding some kind of major mistake to the fundamental wrongness you're suffering!

To be released to any degree from the feeling that you're wrong for feeling something is fundamentally not OK with your whole life can be very freeing indeed!

Yet you might never have thought to cop to all this yourself. Or that copping to it could actually be a signal of your growth and progress as a person, even a religious or spiritual person.

Almost immediately, however, this act of confession also often reveals something of a hitch or glitch in how things are right here at the core. A pattern of potholes in the road of living, or maybe we should say speed bumps. That's what we find in Secret #2.

SECRET #2

It's Really Hard to Be Here, Isn't It?

Let's allow for the possibility that neither your mind, nor your soul, nor your body felt any exhilaration or even quiet relief upon making the confession I suggested in Secret #1.

That's OK. No problem.

A key principle in the discovery of great relief, or even any, is that however you are showing up is fundamentally OK. There is no prescribed way to be that is right, true, or holy.

What I do – and don't – mean by saying, "However you are showing up is fundamentally OK." I'm not offering this principle as license to madness and mayhem. I'm offering it as a simple acknowledgment that our lives as they are, with all their limits, faults, frailties, and failings, are not inherently wrong, sinful, or worthy of any kind of condemnation.

Now, from any number of moral, psychological, religious, spiritual, and philosophical perspectives, we might judge all sorts of human behaviors, including our own, to be wrong, sinful, and quite worthy of condemnation. These perspectives are valid on their own terms. Every single day, in all kinds of ways, our mutual society depends on our making and acting upon such judgments.

Murdering one another, for instance, is not a good thing. It's very bad, in fact. Most of us won't put up with it. In civilized societies all over the Earth, anyone who does this terrible thing to another human being can expect to be sought out, judged severely, and made to suffer harsh consequences.

The same is true of all kinds of other acts that our laws and customs hold to be wrong, sinful, and worthy of condemnation and negative consequences. That is as it should and must be. A common social life with any harmony at all is invariably built upon this foundation.

So when I say that "a key principle in the discovery of great relief, or even any, is that however you are showing up is fundamentally OK," I am not making a statement about your behavior and its relative rightness or wrongness in our social order.

I am, instead, making a statement about your life and the existence in you of all the impulses and patterns that you and others might regard as limits, faults, frailties, and failings. Including impulses, which we all have, to do things that violate features of the prevailing social order.

As you read or listen to this book, then, please know I am inviting you to welcome your responses and reactions to be whatever they turn out to be – even if they're negative toward the book, toward me, toward the whole prospect of great relief in the core wound (whatever it might be).

I'd rather have you toss the book into the garbage can in alignment with your own integrity than keep reading it out of fear, obligation, or accommodation of anyone else's desires or expectations, including my own.

This is a reaction-friendly book – within certain social and ecological limits, of course. So it's fine with me if you get annoyed and throw the book into a trashcan. Not preferable, obviously, but something I can tolerate with a certain appreciation, respect, and humor. I won't feel so cheerful if, in outrage over what you've read, you decide to punch someone out or to blow up a city block.

I am suggesting, you see, that there is great potential benefit in allowing whatever your responses and reactions are to come fully to the surface, to feel them deeply, even to act them out in appropriately controlled ways.

A lot of religious and spiritual people, especially – by no means everyone, but many – spend enormous amounts of energy and attention holding back, stifling, and suppressing responses and reactions to events in life. Why? Because their religious or spiritual teachings and practices, as well as all kinds of other authorities starting way back with Mom and Dad, almost invariably tell them they are not supposed to be having these responses and reactions. Or, if they do, then they are supposed to stuff, stifle, and suppress them.

Just for the record, in almost every single religious or spiritual system on Earth there are individuals, groups, and even whole historical lineages of practitioners who take a much more liberal, embracing orientation to such responses and reactions. If you a religious believer or a spiritual practitioner, as described toward the end of our discussion of Secret #1, it might be good for you to check into this. See where your particular faith or school stands on the subject. And find out where you really stand, *yourself.* There may be room in your precepts and practices for a more creative, enlivening, and liberating way of dealing with these phenomena that are so natural in our daily lives. And there may be individuals and schools within your tradition where you'll be welcome to explore that more embracing, non-orthodox approach to practice.

I meanwhile will offer you a way to deal with your responses and reactions that can make your life much more bearable, rich, and ennobling.

The appearance of impulses like lust, rage, envy, and also feelings of worthlessness, confusion, self-loathing, and self-hatred – the list can go on and on, even for any individual – means to many people that there is something fundamentally wrong with them personally. Unfortunately, their religious and spiritual beliefs often convince them that the mere fact that such impulses and feelings come up in them means there is something wrong, sinful, and worthy of condemnation about their own essential life.

We could make an endless list of the interior and exterior IT Wars that plague human beings. As these examples indicate, IT Wars arise from competing values and beliefs, and also competing projections onto both the present and the future.

To start to realize that "It's Never Enough, Is It?," doesn't mean we then lose all values, priorities, beliefs, and hopes. Rather, we simply begin to get the picture that none of them, not a single one of those things we have or want, is ever going to finally, fully, and perfectly satisfy us. Not the things of life, and not even the things of spirit.

What it takes to recognize the not-enough-ness of our ITs. For most people, it takes a long time to realize that any particular IT they seek to grasp or hold on to while surviving here is not sufficient. It takes time to learn that no such IT can provide the satisfaction, bliss, freedom, fulfillment, security, or peace they thought it would.

What that means is that many of us spend years nurturing the feeling that our ITs really are giving us that satisfaction, freedom, comfort, security, or joy that we seek from them. In other words, people are often slow to understand that what they once thought, felt, and experienced to be IT for them is not IT after all.

There are those who would suggest that we actually spend countless lifetimes refining this very understanding, IT after IT after IT, often coming back for repeated bouts of IT-fascination of one kind or another.

Whatever we might say about the whole notion of reincarnation, that suggestion is worth noting. Getting real-life lessons about the insufficiency of our ITs is no small project.

There are those who hold that this lesson-getting is the most essential purpose of our living. That argument also is worth considering.

So, as you read or listen to this book, I want you – within appropriate social and environmental limits you yourself will have to determine – to give permission to whatever responses or reactions naturally come up in you. Let them come to the surface. Get into them. Find out what they are made of, where they're coming from, why they're so strong. They have things to teach you that no one and nothing else ever can.

I'm not talking from on high here. If anything, I am talking from *on low*. I am talking from underneath where we ordinarily suffer and struggle. It may take some time, and a deep comprehension of at least a few of this book's secrets, for you to get a sense of what this might mean.

I've been immersed for a long time in what I gather is a quite uncommon sensitivity and orientation to our shared condition. You could compare this perspective to the view of living cells that bio-scientists can see through a super-magnifying, dark-field microscope. My perspective is a kind of dark-field illumination of the depths of human feeling and being. It's only now becoming possible for numbers of us to fall into this kind of view and on its basis to make our lives saner and happier.

This kamikaze flight of a life. For that reason, you can perhaps see why I won't worry much if, after making the kind of confession I was urging you toward in the last chapter, you felt unmoved, uptight, and maybe even disturbed about it. In this kamikaze flight of a life, people who are a little uptight and disturbed actually allow me to breathe a little easier.

I mean, think of it: We're all hurtling toward death no matter what we do or don't do. Each one of us, in every moment.

The ones who are busy asserting that everything is just fine and dandy, or that they and they alone have the ticket to salvation, freedom, happiness, love, and peace – they're the ones who make me nervous.

Speaking of kamikaze flights: One of the big differences between a kamikaze pilot and most people alive, of course, is that kamikaze pilots intended and planned to die, while we do not. Kamikaze pilots in World War II signed up to fly their planes down the smokestacks of destroyers, aircraft carriers, and other giant ships. They were deliberately trying to kill themselves, for the sake of their cause. Today's suicide bombers are similarly choosing a hoped-for martyrdom over the continuation of life.

Most of us are not doing anything of the sort. No, we are intending and planning to do the exact opposite of deliberate suicide. We are trying hard to stay alive at all costs. More than that, we are trying to make life as pleasing and gratifying as we can. We each have our own yardsticks by which we measure our success. However we go about it, though, we are here to live, not to die.

Yet dying is what we are always actually doing, no matter how well we appear to be surviving. In every moment this is so. Even from the moment we are conceived in our mothers' wombs, this is so.

Perhaps you find this hard to admit. Getting to admit this is another major step in personal and spiritual growth. Why? *Because it's a real but usually unspoken fact of our lives. Admitting it sets us freer than we were before because it grounds us more fully in our actual reality.*

Exercise for Secret #2: Another admission in the mirror.

- Look at yourself in a mirror, eye to eye, as in the exercise for Secret #1
- Now say aloud, "My name is _____ and in every moment, no matter how well I appear to be surviving, *I am dying.* And nothing I can do is ever going to change that central fact of my life."

(Rumor has it that science is within a few decades, maybe even less, of enabling human beings to live almost indefinitely. When the day comes that most of us really will *never die* under any circumstances, if I am still alive you can be sure I will revise this chapter! Until then, I think this exercise is worth a bit of our still very precious time.)

If you did the exercise . . . how do you feel?

If you want to take it further, speak this same mortal fact of your life to a loved one or friend, as in the exercise for Secret #1.

And – the results?

Journaling on Secret #2 so far. If you like, record your immediate responses and reactions to the exercise(s) you performed just now.

Knowing that we're dying makes it really hard to be here. To admit, especially aloud and directly to another human being, that we are already dying in every moment of living is to enter a harsh realm of, you may have guessed it, paradoxes. Not conceptual paradoxes, not mental riddles and mystifying puzzles. No, this is the world of concrete contradiction. Whatever we are feeling, thinking, and doing, this, I propose, is where we are always *living*.

This particular living paradox – that we're dying all along while we're living – is part of what makes it so very hard to be here in this life.

Have you ever felt this? That it's just really hard to be here? If you're not sure, and even if you are, please take a breath.

Give yourself permission just to acknowledge this: *It is really hard to be here.*

The fact is, it takes enormous, systematic effort just to sustain life in one of these human bodies. What's worse, no matter how hard we try, sooner or later the effort fails. Bodily, we know that death is going to be the outcome of our efforts to stay alive.

We *always* know this.

Consider the implications of that foreknowledge – that we are always dying, and no matter how hard we try to put it off or elude it, we are going to fail, *and we are going to die.*

That foreknowledge is a lot more than a pothole or speed bump (gently suggestive metaphors I used for it at the end of Secret #1). It's more like a brick wall we're hurtling toward that we cannot evade. Or a constant inhibitor, a governor on any and every accelerator of enthusiastic participation in our lives.

Here's another way to look at this situation. How do we relate to knowing we are going to fail at anything in life that we want to achieve? If, in advance and in every moment of trying to accomplish something, anything, we already know we're going to fail, doesn't that knowledge sabotage or at least cut into our energy to succeed?

The underlying feeling/thinking goes something like this: "What's the point? Why am I even doing this? This is absurd. I'm wasting my time, my energy, my life here. This is ridiculous. There is no way I can pull this thing off – yet I'm trying to do it anyway. *What is wrong with me?*"

What if just such a current of bewilderment and despair underlies all of the other currents of our feeling and thinking in daily life? And what if this current is part of the body's innate intelligence all along?

The mind can appear not to notice or understand the body's mortality. But the body is swept up in a continual effort to thwart and fend off death from the moment of conception. It can never afford not to be noticing this. It doesn't have to try. To be aware that it is dying is innate to the body. That noticing is part of its natural intelligence.

A startling illustration of how the body's knowledge communicates itself to the mind occurs whenever a child first learns about death – through the death of a pet, a human relative, a wild creature. Do you remember when you first learned that people die, pets die? Or, if not, have you ever seen a child in the moments of learning this?

Nobody ever gets over learning such a thing. No *body* does.

But the learning – the acquiring of a knowing that was not there before – actually belongs to the emerging mind or psyche, not so much to the body itself. The cellular body-organism is a vast field of continual birthings and dyings. In its instinctual, knowing livingness, the body already and inherently knows it is dying.

Maybe this whole conversation doesn't altogether ring true to you. That's OK. If that's so, let's allow this particular secret I'm putting forward to stand as an unsettled argument or field of non-clarity between us. As I said earlier, I can handle the uneasiness around that, and I assume you can, too.

If it does ring true, then along with me you're feeling at least a quiet un-ease anyway.

Either way, it's really hard to be here.

Let's take another breath.

Whenever I do my version of that exercise, I especially need to tense and relax muscles in my right upper back and lower neck, near my spine. I was rear-ended at a stoplight here in our town late in the year 2000, and for some of my writing time on this book I was suffering a minor whiplash. Even though I've since healed, those tissues still tend to knot up quickly.

So if, like me, taking a breath reminds you of some part of your body that's especially tense or achy, by all means give yourself a little massage. Get up, move around, stretch. This kind of work, and it is *work*, can be tough going for these fragile, pressurized organisms. Let's take it easy on them. . . . Are you sure you don't need to get up and take a break?

We were talking about how the body always, *always* knows it's dying, even from the moment of conception. How that makes it very hard to be here.

But it's not hard to be here only because we're dying while alive. To me, that is the underlying, overarching, all-encompassing *context* of how hard it truly is to be here. Then there are the *content*-filled particulars.

Setbacks also make it really hard to be here. If you're reading this book, life must have dealt you a few blows here and there. Somewhere, somehow, you must have suffered one or more powerful setbacks. Maybe even traumatic ones.

The eventual ending of material life is one thing. Setbacks in the midst of our living are quite another.

"Setback" is an interesting word to contemplate. Look at it in terms of simple physics of motion.

Would you agree that, just to be here, you have had to dare to move forward in all kinds of ways? And, in the midst of those daring attempts to go forward, have you not experienced setbacks?

In the tests of living, the "I" of you, the central force of your identity and being, is trying to move more fully into life. It's as if you can't just sit still, not if you are going to be here as who you really are. You have to keep stepping forward.

In the experience of a setback, the central, forward-moving force of who you are gets knocked back. You know how it feels. Whatever the setback – a time when a parent yelled at you, a betrayal in love, the failure of an enterprise, a loss in a competition, terrible news about someone dear – it's as if the wind gets knocked out of you. You go into a kind of shock.

That central force, which wants to keep moving forward, feels instead as if it were thrown back somewhere into the recesses of your insides. It may feel broken, shattered, and paralyzed, or even devastated, destroyed.*

Moments of setback are times when it's harder than ever to be here. So are moments or periods when we just feel we cannot move forward in a way that does justice to our efforts.

---

* One of my planned sequels to *Great Relief* is tentatively titled, *Great Relief for Broken Souls – And for the Broken Zones in Every Body's Psyche.* If this title touches a chord in you, if you have a sense of being somewhat or terribly broken, shattered, severely ungrounded and diffuse, or pressed way, way back inside yourself much if not most or even all the time, please keep your eye out for this forthcoming book. I've learned not to promise these things by any specific date, but I will try to get that book into your hands as soon as I can.

More journaling on Secret #2. This might be a good time to jot down some further thoughts and feelings about how both your own inevitable dying and your personal experience of setbacks make it hard for you, yourself, to be here.

Conclusion – the great relief we can find in Secret #2.
Remember Matt, the young man I told you about in Secret #1
who committed suicide? He jumped off a bridge just weeks before
his thirty-first birthday. Others later told me bits and pieces of his
final conversations and stories of how depressed he was for a long
time. They gave me the feeling that, after years of not succeeding
as he felt he should have been, taking his own life was for Matt a
final, bitter victory.

Matt was talented, sensitive, and bright. But I gather he
felt there was no real room for him in this world. I get the sense
that he felt excluded from his own life – even though he was
much loved and appreciated. It's possible no amount of love and
appreciation could ever have been enough for him. He had set
standards and criteria to justify his life that love and appreciation
from others could never satisfy.

Because we suffer setbacks and failures to move forward no
matter how hard we try, because we are dying even while we are
living – for these and other "becauses," it's really hard to be here.
That's Secret #2. The feeling that it's really hard to be here is one
of the most primal and universal ways we each register the core
wound of our lives.

I have stated this secret to groups of people in workshops.
It's as if the vocal, outward announcement of this otherwise-
obvious reality lifts a weight off most people's chests. In the mass
media's fascination with super-successful, powerful, beautiful,
wealthy, talented people, and in so much of the conditioning we
receive from parents, religious teachings, spiritual guides, and
philosophies, there's a potent, if often only implicit, but practically
universal suggestion that contradicts this secret.

It goes like this: "If you're really doing life right, why, hey,
it should be easy to be here! *And if you're not cool, if you don't have
your act together, if being here is not a piece of cake for you . . . well,
you must not have much of a clue what it's all about!*"

That propagandistic suggestion hangs on our chests and our shoulders like an invisible vat of concrete. This book offers a small and perhaps aggravating proposition to the contrary. (If you saw Peter Falk's rumpled, mumbling, bumbling but often dead-on accurate detective on American TV, I sometimes feel like the "Colombo" of writers on these things.) I'm offering an irritating but potentially much-relieving suggestion that you dig a little deeper. Scratch their surface a tiny bit, and you see that even those "really-together" people either already know or sooner or later discover a secret that's so obvious and so painful it escapes our view for most of a lifetime:

It's really hard to be here.

For every body.

Period.

If any body hasn't already been numbed and stung by setbacks, still, every single human body knows or fears they're coming.

And sooner or later, to date, every single body loses the fight and is no longer here.

Why?

Not because it, that bodily person, wanted to die. Not really.

No, just simply because it finally got too hard to be here.

You might try reading this last italicized section aloud a few times. Between readings think of everyone you know, perhaps especially the ones who look like they've got it all together. Just feel into this secret. Let its great relief sink in.

It's really hard to be here.

Period.

That's Secret #2.

Secret #3 proposes that even when the events of living make being here relatively easy or attractive . . . something's still missing. Or, whatever we have, and know, and are, "it's never enough."

[T]he core wound . . . . is not sin. It is not a primordial fall from Grace. It is not evil. It is not the devil's work. It is the preliminary, makeshift, inevitable result of the appearance of a life-form on Earth that is as finite as a stone and as infinite as a god. If we step back and look at this event called human being through the lens of long cosmic time, these several thousand years – maybe, according to some, several hundred thousand years – during which humanity has been suffering existence as the core wound, our chronic confusion and separateness are quite understandable. We are having a hard time getting here. We are struggling to clarify our nature. And in the meantime, and in the midst of all our efforts of every kind, there is a great motivating bewilderment, pain, anxiety, craving, yearning, and aspiration: the core wound.

– Saniel Bonder, *Waking Down*

SECRET #3

It's Never Enough, Is It?

Several years ago I heard of a renowned medical specialist who had been exposed to my teachings in the manuscript of this book. This man was an accomplished allopathic physician with an office near the financial district in downtown San Francisco. He was certainly not a spiritual seeker in any obvious way. He never gave any impression of having significant religious feeling or faith. Nor did he appear – at least in the focused activities of his medical science – to have any serious bent toward learning about himself psychologically.

Even so, when he heard the ideas of the core wound and how hard it is to be here, he immediately shared a primary experience of his early life, which was later passed along to me. It touched me so deeply that I am moved to share it here with you.

Even "peak experiences" are never enough. As a boy, the doctor lived in an area of low mountains. At times, he said, he would run to the top of some mountain or other, looking to find at the peak he knew not what, but something, something more, something sufficient.

Yet when he got there, whatever he found or felt, he said, *it was never enough.* Never. Upon returning home, he would tell his mother, in disappointment, "It's not enough. It's just not enough!"

When I heard this story, I was struck by its raw simplicity. It moved me that this accomplished man, a leader in his scientific field, could look at his entire experience and see that, even from his boyhood, life has never given him enough. Whatever it has given, it has never been enough.

I knew that doctor had expressed a secret that, simply admitted, could help a lot of other people enjoy a greater degree of freedom, with greater loving kindness to others as well as to themselves. He inspired me to devote this chapter to that simple secret.

"You mean *this* is IT?!" When one early reader heard my title for this chapter – "It's Never Enough, Is It?" – she said, "Or, 'you mean *this* is IT?!'" I had to laugh. That does say it. How many times have we achieved some sought-after mountaintop, reaching a pinnacle of attainment we had long desired, only then to feel, precisely, "You mean *this* is IT?! This isn't even close to what I thought IT was going to be! This is *not* IT. No way!"

In a later discussion, still another early reader pointed out that it often takes a long time for us to notice the "not-enough-ness" of our various "ITs." He is quite right. This is what makes this particular journey of discovery such a long passage. Just staying alive is of course the big "IT" for these bodies – thus, the effort, energy, and anxiety that forever accompany the act of surviving.

Beyond that, in the living out of life, every human being is also busy seeking, finding, holding onto, or losing all kinds of desired things, events, and connections. A love relationship, a child, money, spiritual experiences, a long vacation, favorite food, drink, or entertainment, intellectual or material success – the list is inexhaustible for us as a species but pretty brief for each individual.

The IT Wars. This particular angle of insight into life can be followed a long way, and it reveals some intriguing views. One, for instance, is the recognition that most human conflict of any kind, whether within an individual or in any form of social relations, can often be boiled down to one simple thing: an "IT War."

People struggle to find or keep the ITs that really work for them – or that they *think* will or do really work for them. To the degree they suffer any ambivalence about what they want in life, they also tend to suffer competing interior arguments on behalf of ITs that are wanting to take them in different directions.

For instance, here in America an astonishing percentage of us are either overweight or clinically obese. Vast numbers of people are thus struggling much of the time between impulses to satisfy their physical hunger (whatever emotions may accompany it) and opposing desires to discipline themselves, eat little or nothing at all or none of the foods they want, exercise more, follow their diets, and so on. One IT is the pleasure that comes from eating, and another IT is the satisfaction that comes from resisting the desire to eat.

That's an example of our many internal IT Wars.

Externally, in relationships, we endlessly tussle over which IT is the best and whose should "win." All our judgments, disputes, and contentions – IT Wars. A couple of examples:

- Religious conflicts are IT Wars. People hold different beliefs about the nature of God and who is going to get saved how. Those for whom religious faith leads to outward IT Wars are often so fearful or fanatical about the ultimate rightness of their own beliefs that they find it necessary to contend against contrary beliefs of others. Sometimes they find it necessary to contend against the beliefs of others even when those others' beliefs don't outwardly contradict theirs. For instance, they have to overcome the beliefs of others, or convert them, even when those others are willing to live in tolerance and mutual respect toward them. Their experience and idea of God or Spirit are such primary ITs to them that they feel the only way they can properly have, serve, or honor those ITs is by making sure as many other people come around to their views as possible. Human history is filled with the carnage of religious IT Wars. It's not a pretty picture – but that is not really the point here. The point here is simply to note how driven people can be by religious ITs.

• A woman's internal distress over, say, whether to seek a promotion at her job, is an IT War. The part of her that feels "don't even try" fears such non-ITs as potential failure to get the promotion and resulting embarrassment and other unpleasant consequences, possible additional stress, extra work hours away from family and more pleasant pastimes if she does get the promotion, and being resented for having dared to go beyond the lot of her co-workers. The part of her that wants to "go for IT" hopes for more income, a higher station in the company and in life, the satisfaction of progress in her career, the enjoyment of greater power including, perhaps, power over those who are presently her peers, and the possibility of getting out from under the bootheel of her current boss. What determines whether she decides to ask for the promotion or not? Her anticipation of which set of conditions will most likely be the most satisfying IT for her. That's all. From this perspective, in the final analysis it's not a matter of destiny, fate, God's will, or any other big-picture determination. She just finds out which IT gets most of her vote for being most likely to make her happy or satisfied in life, and that's what she chooses. (I'm not saying that this perspective is ultimately right or true, by the way; I'm just saying this is how all such choices look through the lens that exposes our IT Wars.)

Journaling Exercise for Secret #3: You and your ITs. Let's combine the exercise and the journaling for this secret. Record some of the ITs you've pinned hopes on during your life and reflect on your adventures with them. Here are some questions you might use as guidelines:

- What led you to feel that any particular IT was going to be enough for you?
- What did "enough" mean for you, exactly?
- What was your experience with that IT?
- When did you conclude that that particular IT was not enough?
- What patterns have you noticed in your life of seeking such ITs or holding on to them?
- What if any ITs are you still seeking or holding on to?

Conclusion – the great relief we can find in Secret #3.
Any thing we can experience, even a spiritual opening into some kind of limitless joy, peace, or unity with God, sooner or later reveals its own limits. When that happens, it ceases to satisfy and fulfill. However, it may take a very long time for that not-enough-ness to become clear. To most people, it apparently never really does, about most of the things they either cling to or seek.

When you start to see the wide-screen vision that no IT can ever fully satisfy you, the great relief available in understanding Secret #3 begins to blossom in your heart and life. But that particular bloom of release may not be at all what you might expect in advance.

Until you start to see that wide-screen vista, yes, there is always something else dangling before you like a carrot from one of two sticks, "the present" or "the future." If some particular IT is dangling from "the present," then you already have IT in your clutches but you are striving to hold on to IT, to keep IT from changing or passing. If the IT is dangling from "the future" – and it might well be something you lost in the past and want to regain – then you are busy seeking for something that is not in your present grasp.

Now some people would say that the goal, then, is to understand that no IT ever satisfies us perfectly and forever, and therefore we should be free of all desire and grasping for or clinging to any ITs whatsoever. Which of course is a superhuman condition of indifference that most human beings are totally incapable of ever realizing. So we would then be setting up an ultimate IT. "The Mother of All ITs." The IT of ITs. The One IT that surpasses all other possible ITs. And we would be superimposing a quest for that ultimate IT of perfect "IT-lessness" on top of our pesky, persistent, unrelenting drive to get or keep ITs of all kinds, physical, emotional, mental, psychic, and spiritual.

This superimposed search for the ultimate IT, in turn, would lead to far more suffering, distress, and dis-ease, and anything but great relief. Wouldn't it?

However, that is not the direction for us to go here. It's the direction of renunciate spirituality – the motto of which, in so many spiritual traditions around the world, is something like, "Let go of everything, of all desire and grasping, and become perfectly indifferent – that is ultimate freedom or at least the gateway to it. Or, rather, to *IT*."

Well, I'm not suggesting that the relief available through grasping Secret #3 is anything like such superhuman spiritual renunciation. I'm proposing something much simpler, humbler, and presently more realistic for nearly all human beings who will ever read or listen to these words – myself included.

I'm saying, rather, that the great relief you and I can enjoy through comprehending Secret #3 is another living paradox. Here it is:

Even though it's true that no IT can ever fully satisfy or fulfill us, *it's the nature of human life to go on clinging to ITs we have and seeking ITs we don't yet have.*

This is so even when we know now, and will know at all times in the future, that our ITs don't absolutely do "IT" for us and never can!

Here's a tender personal example. My wife Linda literally means more to me than anyone else in the whole world. I call her my "Precious Treasure" and I mean it.

Now, I know very well, and so does she, that someday we will lose one another. That's a given. It's just the way it is here.

Yet I cannot help but cling to her in all kinds of ways. I cherish her and our precious time together, even though I know our relationship here in this world is an IT that I will someday lose. And I also know, and so does she, that we are limited beings. Our love has its limits. We long since outgrew the naïve insistence that somehow anyone, including either one of us, could themselves always satisfy us perfectly.

So – is there an IT here that I cling to, in loving Linda?

Absolutely.

Am I trying to stop clinging to her so I can supposedly be more free?

Absolutely not.

Am I therefore setting myself up for an eventual terrible loss and disappointment?

Absolutely.

Based on this recognition, should I therefore be trying to rid myself of the habit of clinging to this IT of our love and Linda's presence in my life?

No way!

Instead, I just get to live in the admission that even this IT is not enough – because I can't either perfect our love to some absolute degree or perpetuate our present human lives into eternity – while continuing to cling to IT, in other words loving her so much, every moment of every day.

Do you get the picture? Even *after* you see the wide-screen view that no IT can ever fully satisfy you, well, yes, *even then*, there is always something else dangling before you like a carrot from one of two sticks, "the present" or "the future." And you're always holding and protecting, or reaching and grasping. Just like I said above about what life is like before you understand this secret.

The relief is in the knowing, and the accepting, even in every cell of your body, that that's just the way it is. That's the deal. That's life. And it's not vulnerable to heroic efforts to stomp it out, either material, religious, or spiritual. This "way-it-is-ness" is not going to disappear perfectly on the basis of any efforts you can ever make.

I realize that this contention flies in the face of much cherished religious, spiritual, and even secular philosophy. Well, I did say that the great relief you find here might well require you to reevaluate some of your beliefs. More than that, it might move you to find a larger view of reality, one that can contain features of how life is that now appear to oppose or exclude one another.

That's the paradoxical freeing up, and a great relief indeed, that shows up when we let the full import of Secret #3 come home to roost in our hearts like a long-lost homing pigeon.

It's never enough, is IT?

And that homecoming, felt to any degree at all, leads to a series of other, equally paradoxical recognitions and enjoyments of great relief. Like the ones we can find in Secret #4.

SECRET #4

Every Body Is Homeless Here –
Even the Ones Living Under Expensive Roofs

So we're dying in every moment of living, always fending off death just to stay here – but we have to keep moving forward to be here, and life is full of setbacks no matter how hard we try to avoid them. Life is always pushing us back, until at last it pushes us right back out of it. No matter how hard and for how long we push forward to stay here, sooner or later we're back out of the picture. "Exit stage rear." Or we pop out the top. Or fall through a trap door. (Great phrase, "trap door.") One way or another, we're out of here.

In the meantime, whatever life gives us is never enough. No IT we try to hold onto, or seek and ever attain, can truly satisfy us.

I'm not saying all of this is the way life always looks to everybody. Some people appear to be able to be here without moving forward much at all. They find a niche in life and appear content to occupy it without much challenge or complaint.

And, again, some people feel quite satisfied with the ITs they've already got. They don't feel disturbed by the potential loss of any of those things in any moment, or by their inevitable loss of all earthly things in death.

If you're reading or listening to this book, that last paragraph probably doesn't describe you. My hunch is that you're one of the serious, inquisitive, and agitated. One of the dissatisfied. Perhaps a despairing and therefore desperate character, even if only a hidden one.

Famous and glamorous people can be desperate, too. You never know who might be among the truly desperate. A few years ago I read in a paper a striking little article about Jane Fonda.

Here is a household-word, brand-name celebrity who needs no introduction beyond her name itself. Many of us have known about Jane Fonda since our childhood or teenage years, in my case at least several decades ago. She has led one of the most glamorous, dramatic, visible lives of our time.

Early on Fonda built upon her Hollywood pedigree as Henry Fonda's daughter to become a movie star herself, and eventually a serious actress. She's had a succession of extraordinary men in her life, including a famous director (Roger Vadim), a famous leftist radical turned politician (Tom Hayden), and one of the wealthiest men of our time (Ted Turner). She's taken some strong stands, starting with anti-Viet Nam war activities that earned her approval from some quarters and strong objections and even notoriety from others. Later she made a name for herself as a successful teacher of aerobic and yogic exercise, especially for other women. More recently she's become the director of a non-profit organization that helps inner city young women find alternatives to early pregnancy and motherhood as avenues of self-esteem. A primary cause of her divorce from Ted Turner was that she became a devout Christian.

Knowing such things about her, one would think that if anyone on this Earth might have had a rewarding, enriching, exciting life – challenging, yes, but fundamentally positive, and certainly free of crippling self-doubt and desperate internal struggle – Jane Fonda would be such a person.

But in this article I read, Jane Fonda was stepping out of the closet with a secret she had kept hidden, apparently, for more than a quarter of a century. She was admitting that she has struggled all along with anorexia and bulimia.

In the article she made a telling confession about what life was like for her all that time. Fonda said that for those twenty-five years, *she was never able to take even a single bite of food without suffering intense fear.*

Feel into that. Whatever your personal or political opinions of Jane Fonda, for a moment just feel into what this must have been like for her as a fellow human being. Feel what that kind of terror must do to one's life, no matter what other wonderful or glamorous qualities that life might have. Imagine living that way – unless you already do and don't have to imagine it!

Whatever we may be suffering, most of us do not have to live with such naked fear every time we take a bite of food. Not to mention the inevitable shame and other kinds of distress that surely come with it, as long as we cannot openly admit our suffering and seek help.

Every time a celebrity like Jane Fonda makes such a public announcement of a personal struggle with a serious addiction, everyone else who suffers it gets to breathe a sigh of relief. So does everyone who suffers anything like it. Yes, some particularly hardened hearts might take pleasure in the exposure of a celebrity's feet of clay. But for most people, knowing that one of our human "stars" is contending with the same stress and anguish they themselves do makes it a little easier to be here on Earth.

And that star's own messiness, vulnerability, and weakness make our hearts go out to her, or him. I admire Fonda for her honesty and openness, and especially her courage in admitting the stark fear that attended her every taste of food for a quarter century.

All that time, then, Jane Fonda was among the truly desperate. You just never know.

This book is for the homeless – whether or not they live under expensive roofs. Once, at a workshop I was leading, I read aloud portions of an earlier draft of this book. When I'd finished, one young woman took issue with some of the points I brought up in Secret #2, "It's Really Hard to Be Here, Isn't It?"

She said that she has a different relationship to the fact of bodily mortality than what I was describing. Yes, she said, she understands it's very hard to be here. She knows she is dying, that life is slipping past.

But all of that only gives her all the more passion to make the most of every day. It keeps her focused and intent on enjoying life to the fullest. It doesn't move her to despair. Rather, it motivates her to really give herself over into every moment of her living.

I replied that I'm sure there are many people who feel similarly, but they are not the ones to whom I am addressing this book. Not primarily, anyway.

As it so happened, this woman had already passed through a fundamental healing in her own being. She was already enjoying a powerful liberation from the primal anxiety at the core of life that distresses nearly every human body on Earth. Automatically, then, her disposition relieved her of a certain level of need for what this book offers.

Many people who have not gone through such a fundamental healing nonetheless share her orientation. Indeed, many people who share her basic drive to make the most of life would not be attracted to a book with this title. It wouldn't occur to them that they have any need whatsoever for "great relief." They wouldn't even be able to relate to the concept. All of this would seem silly to them, superfluous, self-indulgent. They'd be saying, "Get a life! Get a job. Get your act together. Stop whining!"

People who are not hungry for a most fundamental, pervasive change at the core of their lives aren't likely to partake of what I'm offering here.

Apart from the ones who just can't relate, some are already full or are happily eating from another plate. The woman I was speaking with was perhaps one of these. They might say they have gone or are going beyond the need for such an offering. And they'd be right.

However, there are also countless people who don't have the juice to make the most of life. They don't have the confidence, the energy, the hope. They are beaten down by experience, broken even. They are the ones who live in "quiet desperation."

Some of these are literally homeless, down and out, on the streets.

Others are the homeless who live under expensive roofs, drive nice cars, and surround themselves with all kinds of fine things. But they feel, if not an immense black hole at the core of their existence, then certainly an emptiness, malaise, purposelessness, an indefinable dissatisfaction that nothing positive can touch.

The "homeless under expensive roofs" would also include many of the Jane Fondas of our world. These folks suffer a bizarre twist to their anguish. They have their lives together in so many obvious ways – talk about "making the most of life!" Yet they live in secret terror and shame, shattered by traits or syndromes over which they have no control. They're so crippled by what they suffer that they can't yet even speak about it, much less ask for help and seriously begin the long, hard walk on the path to healing.

Meanwhile, to others, sometimes even their spouses, everything looks fine. They lead lives that appear to be enviable in almost every possible way. In fact, they look like real experts at being here. They appear happy both with what they've got, which is plenty, and with the challenges of getting more. Unlike 99% of the rest of us, they already know they are sure to succeed. At least, that's how they look.

Underneath, however, they're sweating blood. They secretly suspect or know their glamorous A-list lives are just a sham. And they don't have a clue what to do about it. Even doing noble, charitable deeds doesn't change how they feel at the core. The better they get at looking like they're making the most of life, the emptier they feel, and the more they secretly despair.

If you are one of the homeless bodies, the last thing you need from me is a pep talk. Whatever your own predicament, whether you are literally down and out or surviving desperately under an expensive roof, I know you homeless bodies are out there. I hope you have found this book and are reading or listening to this passage right now.

The last thing you need from me is some cheery pep talk about how to milk the most out of every moment of your life.

If you are this desperate, you probably don't even know how to eat or, speaking of milk, how to "drink" any more.

You may wonder if you even really have a mouth to open for this kind of milk.

You may well feel that the most you can get yourself to do is just read or listen to these writings.

You may question why you even go on living at all.

Unlike most people who write books about such things, I don't have any immediate answers for you. Nor any guarantees that what I am writing even *can* make a real difference for you.

All I can say here is, *I* am aware of *you*. Not by name, not in some woo-woo psychic intrusion on the privacy of your soul – but in an essential, simple, and unmistakable way, I feel you. And I honor the relentless heat and roar of the flames in your private hell. I know that at times, even most of the time, that superheating roar makes it damn near impossible to hear what anyone else is saying.

In that feeling, knowing awareness, I am holding you. That is, I am consciously acknowledging the "space" that you uniquely occupy in this human world. I'm quite aware of your homelessness here. Sometimes that awareness makes my own heart ache so much for you, it brings me to tears. I can't begin to pretend that motivational inspirations will have any relevance for you whatsoever.

If anything might be remotely of help to you, it is for me to bow my head in the direction of your particular hell and – at least with respect to pep talks – keep my mouth shut.*

So, I replied with some emotion to my young friend that day at our retreat that people who are enthusiastic, who are jazzed to make the most of life in any way, are not likely candidates for finding great relief in these bodily secrets to freedom, love, and trust. Not in the ways I'm describing. And, with the rare exceptions of those who have already done so, they're not likely candidates for hearing about the core wound of their lives and what they can and can't do about it.

Spiritual seekers: "despairing" or merely "unfinished"?
In what I read aloud that day I also referred to spiritual seekers who are despairing of ever fulfilling their quests. One of the other participants told me that he wondered whether many seekers would connect with that description.

As it happened, like the woman who first spoke, he also had recently completed a fundamental healing and awakening at the core of his being. But he could still speak from personal experience of what it was like for him before that transformation.

He remembered that, before that time, he did not feel that he was despairing so much as incomplete. His search was not yet finished. Something else was required; what, he did not know.

When he found the process of spiritual awakening I offer, he fell into that "what." That falling ended his spiritual search.

---

* Though I'll be touching on these painful depths of our suffering and bewilderment elsewhere in this book, again, as I mentioned in a note in Secret #2, please look for my forthcoming addition to this series, to be titled, *Great Relief for Broken Souls – And for the Broken Zones in Every Body's Psyche.*

His point, as we talked there at the workshop, was that many seekers like him might better respond to descriptions of themselves as "incomplete" or "unfinished" rather than "despairing." I agreed. He's probably right. There are all kinds of ways to be here, and unfinished seeking is definitely a popular mode in some circles, if not exactly a preferable one!

At the beginning of this book, I mentioned that several different kinds of people would likely experience different qualities of great relief. I spoke of everyday heroes, religious believers, and spiritual practitioners. Among the latter category I also acknowledged frustrated spiritual seekers. In this yet smaller population segment, I expect some people would freely describe themselves as "desperate" or "burned out" while for others terms like "unfinished" or "uncompleted" would feel closer to home.

Part of the reason I am bringing up such people here is because on some level they might seem to be the total opposite of the inwardly desperate characters we were considering above. To those who are devastated inside no matter what their outward lives look like – the homeless, under whatever kind of roof or none at all – the notion of being a basically happy but yet vaguely "unfinished" spiritual meditator or seeker has got to be wildly imaginative. It's like a description of a member of a different species.

If you yourself identify with that description – an unfinished seeker rather than a despairing one – let me ask you a question. In your exploration of this book so far, have you been able to identify with a fundamental anxiety or even simple listlessness at the core of your existence? With how difficult it is to be here? With the insufficiency of any and every IT that you can have, or know, or experience?

Do you also sense that there may yet be a reservoir of anguish underneath or perhaps hidden from that part of yourself that feels close to spiritual oneness with infinite being?

I'm not implying that "yes" is the true answer to these questions for everybody. Whatever your true answers are, good! At the same time, I am confident that many unfinished seekers will likely find a big "yes" to these questions about what may lurk underneath their relatively serene feelings of spiritual incompleteness.

Every body is a frustrated spiritual seeker. Recognizing the effectiveness of the Alcoholics Anonymous program, the great psychologist Carl Jung made the comment that all alcoholics are frustrated spiritual seekers. He held that their only hope for permanent recovery lay in finding authentic spiritual experience or understanding.

I want to take that orientation a few steps further. I suggest that every *body* is a frustrated spiritual seeker. (When I say "every," I acknowledge that perhaps a few hundred or a few thousand out of six billion are no longer frustrated seekers. They amount to a minuscule percentage of us indeed. So the term "every," if not precise, is true enough to be used.)

Every body is looking for his, her, its true home. That home cannot be found merely in authentic spiritual or transcendent experience. Spiritual awakening is crucial for many, yes. But it must also be integrated with an extraordinary enlivening of and identification with our ordinary bodies, feelings, and personalities. We've got to bring spirit down to Earth. We've got to weave it into the world of kids, mortgages, deaths in the family, lines on the face, all the challenges and degradations of well-being that we open ourselves to every time our eyelids first lift to the next new day.

Spiritual experience by itself almost invariably tilts an imbalance in our lives. Yes, it moves us out of being so painfully identified with our limited body (and its limited mind). That can be quite healthful. But such spiritual experience can also move us into an opposite concentration. When it does, we become identified either with limitless spirit or with a passionate quest for union with that spirit. We move out of one form of imbalance, then, and into another.

The whole worldview that divides life up into "spiritual" and "non-spiritual" or "sacred" and "profane" is built upon the fundamental wrongness, illness, or lack this book is addressing. It's built upon a most primal split at the core of our existence.*

Every body is homeless here.

Every body is bereft of knowing, living, easily and always being with its own essence of undying spirit.

Every heart is anxious, even desperate, to get relief from a chronic, unnameable distress.

Incomplete or unfinished seekers are, in almost every case, tilted way over toward spirit. They're identifying with spirit to the exclusion of identifying with the body – or, they're trying to become one with spirit that way, at all costs. They're way out of both balance and what I would describe as true integrity. If the essential parts of our being are chronically dis-integrated, split off from each other, somehow opposed, even in conflict or at war, true integrity cannot exist. Why? Because that integrity is not just an expression of honesty and sincerity, or of being reliably true only to one, predominating part of a severely fragmented being.

Over the years I have learned that real healing (which means "wholing") of our lives begins with a realistic estimation of the plight not of the soul, but of the body. Once we've come further down into the body, then and only then will we begin to be able to grasp the plight of the soul. And only then will we become capable of true integrity.

––––––––––––––––––

* Please also see my brief book of interviews and short essays, *Healing the Spirit/Matter Split: An Invitation to Wake Down in Mutuality and Fulfill Your Divinely Human Destiny* (Mt. Tam Empowerments, 2004).

Exercise for Secret #4: Making room for your own homelessness. It may be wise now to do something physical that can help you feel the homelessness I am describing. That homelessness is something we're always in contact with at the deepest places in our very being. But it's not something we are always or even often deeply feeling. It's good to get in contact with that feeling. I'm not saying, by the way, that it's necessary or even good to always be plunged into that feeling – just that it's good to get in contact with it.

Before I present the exercise, let me offer a disclaimer: If your personal experience of "home," especially in early life, has been of a place of danger, terror, and abuse, you may not connect with "homelessness" in the manner I'm inviting you to here. "Homelessness" might instead mean freedom and immunity to continual insanity and threats to your well-being! Some participants at one of my "Great Relief Workshops" said it worked better for them to approach this exercise rather as a way of getting in touch with how "exposed" every body really always is in this life. If that approach strikes a chord in you, feel free to take it as you go through this exercise.

Here it is:

- Wherever you are right now, take your body out of any safe enclosure
- If you are reading or listening at home, stand up and go outside for a moment without adding or taking off any clothing (unless you're naked or nearly so, of course), and close the door behind you
- If you're in your car, stop as soon as you can, park, get out, and close the door behind you
- If you're already outdoors, then if you're in a relatively protected place, leave it and enter a relatively unprotected place

The point is not to put yourself in actual danger, but to enter a more exposed physical environment.

- NOW: Imagine you can't go back to your home, your car, your protected place
- Imagine you are stuck out in the elements, with only the clothes on your back, and no home anywhere
- Imagine this is how it's going to be for you for the rest of your life

Here's the tricky part:

- NOW: Give yourself permission to grasp that this is really how it always is for you, *bodily*
- Let the intuitive feeling settle deep inside you that as a living, human body, *you are always homeless here* in this life, always exposed to all kinds of threats to your well-being and nurturance in this dangerous world
- Look back at the door of your home or your car, or at the entrance to whatever safer enclosure you emerged from
- Feel into this question: When you go back inside, will that enclosure give you the reality of ongoing safety, protection, and *home?* Or will it only give you an *appearance* of these things?
- Go back inside, and . . .
- See how you feel now

Journaling for Secret #4. Write down whatever you feel is worth recording about how this exercise affected you. How does this presentation of Secret #4 strike you altogether? Where is it taking you? What feelings is it bringing up, if any?

While your responses and reactions are fresh, write them down, including any questions they may bring up about where all this is leading.

Conclusion – the great relief we can find in Secret #4.
Every body is homeless here – even the ones living under expensive
roofs. Every body is a spiritual seeker. And every life is suffering
some kind of fundamental split, imbalance, or discontinuity at its
core. (If not absolutely *every single one,* then very nearly so!)

Finding true home requires a healing of that essential split,
imbalance, and discontinuity in our being.

Before we can take the cure, however, we've got to refine our
diagnosis of our illness. We've got to know what it is, exactly, that
we suffer.

Is it some kind of "original sin"? I don't think so.

Have we made a horrible mistake simply by being born?
Again, I think not.

But we do appear to be suffering a primal illness. Again, I
call it "the core wound." It's not really an illness. I'd say, rather,
that the way we are chronically related to our core wound is
"ill-ing," unsettled and unsettling. It tends to perpetuate certain
symptoms of distress from the essential center of our lives.

A few moments ago, when introducing the Exercise for
Secret #4, I said it's good to be able to get into contact with how
that homelessness or sense of exposure we all suffer really feels,
deep inside. I also said it's neither necessary nor good to always be
plunged into that kind of feeling. This perhaps goes against the
grain of some teachings or healing methods you may know of.
Those teachings and techniques would tend to make you feel that
in order to really deal with this current of feeling, you've got to be
practically drowning in it all the time.

My motto is, "No unnecessary pain." The real process of
growth and healing provides necessary doses of pain without our
going looking for them. If you're out of touch with those "places"
in your own life and heart, it's good to know how to take a jump
into those deep waters. If you feel like you're drowning in them
already, it's actually better to learn how to find some solid ground

under your feet. Which is the intended effect of this secret for you, and so many others. By appreciating each secret, different people get unburdened in their own ways as they become more fully sensitized to and in the core wound of their life.

For those reasons, the great relief you may be finding in Secret #4 is essentially whatever it means for you, personally, to get, a little bit closer to the bone than you may ever have before, that every body is homeless and exposed here – especially you. Not "especially you" more than anybody else. No, "especially you" simply because you are in a position to appreciate your body's homelessness here far more than anybody else is. And you're also in a position to appreciate your own bodily exposure far more than anybody else's.

This pervasive insecurity and shelterlessness is one of the defining characteristics of the core wound of your life – and of every body's life. Allowing yourself to acknowledge that fact, if you can, brings a certain peace. Perhaps a disillusionment too, which at first carries some sadness, but soon resonates with dignity and strength. Shedding illusions, after all, sets us free and gives us clarity and power.

I realize you may be getting antsy to just hear already exactly what the core wound is. May I request your continued patience? That definition, coming in Secret #8, is something like the mountaintop of this book. Everything we explore beforehand takes us up to a real readiness to make that clarifying ascent. And what we look into afterward in Secret #9 will naturally take us down, like flowing water, into another landscape of healing wisdom. New, unexplored territory on the continent of your life – which will continue opening before you after you complete and close this book.

Perhaps you're noticing that you are more than antsy. You may even feel anxious about all this, or perhaps "about" nothing at all. Just anxious. That takes us straight into Secret #5.

SECRET #5

Every Body Has an Anxious Heart

When I say it's hard for us to be here (Secret #2), I don't mean it's hard to be here *in* these bodies. I mean it's hard to *be* these bodies. You are not merely "in" your body (or "out of your body," either). You *are* your body.

I was speaking along similar lines at the end of Secret #4, just above – referring to your body's homelessness and your own as if they were the same thing.

They are.

We'll work on this distinction here in Secret #5 – that you're not just *in* your body, but you *are* your body.

At the moment I want to draw our attention once again to the sheer biological pressure every body is under just to survive. Whatever may be true about the soul and its possible survival after the body's death, no body can seriously deny that it is going to die. Every body knows that sooner or later, its death is inevitable.

It has been said that fear of death is the beginning of wisdom. But human history amply demonstrates that fear of death has been the beginning of all kinds of foolishness as well.

Some would say, rather, that accepting the inevitability of death is the beginning of true wisdom. And they might argue that deep acceptance overcomes the fear.

All such notions appear to me to be products of minds that are trying to fix or dispel the primal anxiety we suffer around our physical mortality. There is a simpler and more fundamental way to relate to all this. It confers a wisdom all its own.

That way begins with acknowledging that our bodily hearts – those central muscles of our survival – are always anxious.

If you can agree even provisionally that you are *being* your body, then it's not just that you *have* an anxious heart. You *are* an anxious heart.

There's nothing wrong with being an anxious heart. On the contrary, I suggest it's unnatural, unrealistic, even wildly idealistic to assume there is something wrong with feeling anxious at the core of bodily life.

To help bring this point home, I'd like to suggest a couple of exercises that I think it's important for you to actually do. In other words, please don't treat this exercise sequence as optional.

Exercise for Secret #5: Making two provisional agreements about *being* your body and its anxious heart. A moment ago I spoke of agreeing provisionally that you are not just in your body, but you are *being* your body.

For some people this may be obvious. "Of course I *am* my body, I'm being my body. How could I not be? That's like asking me to agree that the sky is blue. Of course it is! What's the point?"

For others, though, making that kind of agreement even tentatively can be a stretch. They may deeply believe that, while they *have* a material body, what they *are* is a spiritual soul or even an impersonal spiritual awareness. They may feel that, as such a soul or awareness, they are *in* their bodies, or perhaps are somehow outside their bodies, observing them. But they would find it challenging, if not impossible, to agree that they are *being* those bodies.

In any case, let me approach you about this in a more direct way, without making assumptions.

I'd like to ask you to make two temporary agreements with me, binding only for as long as it takes you to read or listen to this book.

Here's the first one: Will you agree to accept and assume, just while you are reading or listening to this book, that you may indeed be your body? That you are not merely *in* your body – as a mind, self, soul, or awareness that is also strangely separate or alien from it – but that you may also somehow be *being* it?

If you are willing to make this agreement, please state it aloud as follows. You may want to return to the mirror for this exercise:

• "My name is _____ and at least while I am reading *Great Relief,* I agree to accept and assume that I may indeed *be* my body – that I may not merely be 'in' my body, as a mind, self, soul, or awareness that is also somehow alien or separate from that body, but that I may also *be* my body itself."

I am not asking you to believe this. Right now I'm not even asking you to feel how it might be so. Even if your experience and understanding of human nature incline you to assume otherwise, all I need now is your mental agreement that it *may* be so.

The second provisional agreement I'd like you to make with me follows upon the first:

Will you agree, also just while you are reading or listening to this book, that it is quite natural to have an anxious heart, in fact to *be* an anxious heart?

I understand this agreement may appear to go against the very promise of the book itself. After all, aren't I offering you great relief from, among other things, that very anxiety in your heart?

Yes, I am offering you great relief. But the offering does not immediately banish any of that heart-anxiety. On the contrary, the relief comes when you stop fighting against the anxiety and begin, strangely enough, to relax into *being* it. In that shift, your energy and attention are freed up from a previously chronic, futile conflict. Any time energy and attention get set free from chronic, futile activity, you naturally feel some form of relief.

Welcome to another *living* paradox – a mysterious bio-spiritual secret in which apparent opposites seem to merge and become the same thing, while somehow still remaining separate and opposite. Admittedly, this can sound and feel absurd:

When you stop fighting this anxiety and relax into being it, you feel some quality of *relief* from it?

Even while you are still *being* it?

Go figure!

So, even if you find all this pretty confusing now, even if this discussion so far is only making you more anxious, if, despite all that, you are willing to make this temporary, provisional agreement, then please state it aloud:

• "My name is _____ and I agree, provisionally, while I'm investigating *Great Relief,* that it's quite natural to have an anxious heart – in fact, it's quite natural to *be* an anxious heart."

Again, it's ok to make this agreement without either feeling or believing that it's really true. It's provisional, temporary. You're free to decide later, conclusively, that it's not *your truth*. (Later, you're even free to decide it's not true *period* – in any way, shape, or form. That's your business, *later*.)

If you can't make these two provisional agreements for your own sake, but, even so, if this book has prompted you to feel a basic trust of me as a sincere fellow human, then just do it as a temporary favor to me. Entertain these novel possibilities, ok?

You might wonder why I'm harping on this. Well, I do have a plan here. At the moment it feels important to me to get you to state aloud, with your own lips, mouth, and tongue:

"I may indeed *be* my body . . . I may not merely be 'in' my body, as a mind, self, soul, or awareness that is also somehow alien, separate, or at least distinct from that body, but . . . I may also *be* my body itself."

"It's quite natural to have an anxious heart – in fact, it's quite natural to *be* an anxious heart."

Stating these propositions aloud is like trying them on for size. Maybe they won't fit. But maybe they will. And if they do, they may indeed help you comprehend the secrets I'm suggesting your body wants you to know.

The biological struggle of every human heart – enlightened or not. On a most foundational level, every human heart is straining to bear the impact of knowing in advance that it is going to die.

I know of saints whose bodies have radiated to others a tangible, wondrous peace, who have nonetheless died of – maybe you guessed it – heart attacks.

Before those immensely tranquil hearts died, they too struggled to stay alive.

Compared to most stressful, confused, and spiritually unillumined hearts, theirs were uncommonly peaceful even while alive. But I am not talking here about emotional and spiritual tranquility.

I am talking about the energy it takes just to keep the blood pumping through the entire body twenty-four hours a day.

I am talking about the effort it takes just to keep one's living organism safe, sound, and in decent health.

To keep it from disintegrating.

From being invaded by parasitic microbes and viruses.

From starving.

From getting cut, flattened, punctured, skewered, roasted, exploded, strangled, mangled, or drowned.

From being overwhelmed by excruciating pain, whether physical or emotional.

From dying.

Such struggle is natural to human life, perhaps to all life. But it takes its toll. In human beings, at the very least it prompts an unrelenting, primitive, biological anxiety that underlies everything else in our lives. That anxiety has natural psychic components and inevitable consequences. It's a material, emotional, and psychological baseline of human living.

Journaling on Secret #5. Perhaps take a few moments to write down responses to these questions:

- How are those two provisional agreements sitting with you?
- Do you agree that your heart is fundamentally in primal stress or anxiety at all times, no matter how you feel on a more superficial level?
- What feelings and thoughts are coming up in you about all this now?

Conclusion – the great relief we can find in Secret #5.
These hearts and bodies are programmed to die at some point.
Very few of us ever know when that moment will come. Typically
our bodies expire from causes we discover, at best, shortly before
dying. Knowing we are going to die and all it takes to fend it off
as long as possible make every heart and body anxious in a most
primal way all the time – until the death itself.

Please note that I did not title this secret, "Each of Us *Is*
Our Body – and Every Body Has and *Is* an Anxious Heart." I only
asked you to make provisional, temporary agreements with me
that you may be your body and its anxious heart. Even though
that other title I just mentioned may be true enough in the
abstract, for many it would have been difficult or impossible to
work with as an actual reality.

And that in turn might have compromised the great relief
that this secret can, I hope, provide for you.

Even so, those provisional, temporary agreements have a key
purpose. In working with people, I've observed that the mind does
not have to understand this kind and depth of communication in
order for the feeling heart and body to register its basic truth.

If you still can't mentally accept these agreements, that in
itself is probably making you a bit uneasy.

And even if your mind is clear about all this, you may still
be feeling uneasy or distressed.

So, you ask . . . *where's the great relief in that?*

Well, for one thing, when you relax more into feeling what
being alive is like for you, if you come upon some kind of root
anxiety, *that's ok.* That is totally natural.

Your religious or spiritual beliefs or personal convictions
might make you feel you should not have such anxiety – even that
feeling it at all is evidence you are not really relaxing, not being
faithful or practicing correctly, not becoming truly peaceful.

But I am proposing that, from this curious perspective,

encountering that deeper anxiety is encountering your bodily reality. I am suggesting that those contrary beliefs and assumptions may be misleading illusions that divorce you from your actual reality and thus cause unnecessary, additional anxiety and stress. And therefore – paradox! – you may find more joy and simplicity by going through that disillusioning encounter.

Some yogis are said to be able to put their hearts and entire biological lives into suspended animation at will. Whatever that might accomplish for them, however, if they stayed that way, eventually their bodies would still die.

And if they come out of their trances, then, like the rest of us, they benefit by and also suffer the symptoms of having an anxious heart – a heart struggling to guarantee life in the body for one more heartbeat, one more breath, one more moment of living. This struggle contends against many odds that each heart knows, instinctively, will eventually defeat it and in effect "win" the struggle.

So, welcome to the basic ok-ness of having an anxious heart. Welcome to that reality of being a body, of *being* your heart.

I'll repeat it once more, just for us to ponder together:

Even though we may feel alienated or at least separate from our bodies, there is a basic way in which each of us not only has a body but is *being* that body.

And in that sense each of us not only *has* a heart.

Each of us *is being* that heart.

In Secret #6 we'll look more closely at what every body is doing all the time in its efforts to stay alive, whole, and integrated.

For now, take a breath.

And see if there isn't some significant flow of release, a kind of exhalation, in just knowing this: Doing the primitive things that guarantee you can stay alive, your heart is always anxious.

That's just the way it is. There's nothing you or I or anyone else can do to change that.

Every body has an anxious heart.

SECRET #6

Every Body Is Always and Only Equalizing Pressures

While I was finishing the last chapter and looking for a transition into this one, I remembered something from my childhood.

My father was in the garment industry. Born in New York, I grew up mostly in small town North Carolina. Our town was not far from a first factory where he worked as a vice-president and, later, a second, larger one, that he owned and presided over.

I remember going into those plants and marveling at the sheer amount of activity there. Looking back now, it strikes me that if one did not already know what was going on in such a place, it might not be too clear.

Great numbers of people come into the place every day and spend time interacting. There are special places where they eat, other places where they relieve themselves. The place is noisy. It wouldn't appear that talking is a major thing they are there to do together, though sometimes groups gather – sometimes all of them at once – and do a lot of talking.

However, most of the people's interactions don't have to do with each other. They have to do with pieces of cloth. Enormous amounts of the stuff, on giant bolts, get carted into the place through one main door. The people then move it around, make marks on it, cut it up, and run pieces of it through odd, noisy little machines that attach the pieces to one another. Eventually they send completely rearranged versions of the fabric out another main door, into trucks that take it all away. Enormous amounts of discarded material go out yet another door, into big bins. At the end of each day everybody in the place goes out another set of doors and leaves. Only a guard stays there overnight.

If you know that the purpose of the place is to make raincoats that are sent to stores to be sold to other people, all of that activity begins to make unified sense. The place is dedicated to one essential thing: making raincoats for sale.

What are these human "factories" (bodies) doing? If the human body can be considered a kind of factory, with its different parts and organs serving various functions, what one thing is that factory always doing – in every body's case?

There are probably many accurate and appropriate ways of answering that question. Secret #6 offers one such possible answer. This answer appears to be universally true, regardless of who each body is, where and how she or he lives, what he or she thinks and believes, and all other particular details that distinguish that individual from all others.

Here it is:

Every body is always and only equalizing pressures.

In Secret #5 I mentioned saints and spiritual tranquility. We typically think of religious and spiritual quests as pursuits of the soul or the spirit. But, to me, spiritual seeking is just one of the body's ways of equalizing pressures.

The body itself, alive and sentient, is a dynamic structure of limits. To find a form of limitlessness, or less-limitedness, promises relief. It equalizes pressures.

Just being alive in this world – whatever might be the case in other dimensions, if they even exist – is a tight squeeze. We are each always under enormous pressures. And every single thing going on in us, every thing we do, is constantly making adjustments to equalize those pressures.

Sensations communicate one or another kind of pressure to us. We adjust to them according to their relative pleasurableness or painfulness.

Feelings arise in response to both external and internal stimuli, which are themselves functioning as pressures. And we do things – spiritual, mental, psychic, emotional, energetic, or physical – to accommodate and equalize the pressures those feelings prompt in us.

So it also is with our thoughts.

Meanwhile, each human body is a vast biological empire of highly coordinated organisms and processes continually making adjustments to pressures inside and out. This is what every body is doing all day and all night long, every single moment of our lives.

When a living human body feels too cold it seeks heat. When it feels too hot it seeks cooling. When it feels hungry it seeks food. When it feels full it stops eating. Then it puts that food through a digestive process which itself is dealing with the pressure of a continual need for various nutrients. Finally it produces an internal pressure that prompts it to excrete wastes.

When it needs to give and receive love, it seeks special forms of contact with other humans or other living creatures. When it feels a lack of mental or spiritual nourishment, it seeks different kinds of contact. It exposes its senses, mind, heart, or spirit to sources of mental or subtle influence. In the manner I am speaking of here, these influences are also pressures, and the impulse to seek them out is also a response to pressures and is itself a pressure.

If we understand that human organisms experience pressure and lack of pressure across a broad spectrum of potential phenomena, ranging from the sheerly material to the purely spiritual, then it begins to become obvious that every human body is always and only equalizing pressures.

(From this perspective, by the way, we can look again at a garment manufacturing plant and see that its entire function is to equalize pressures as well. All the things that enter the building from without – the people and the giant bolts of cloth – are enfolded into a process that expels both later, each in its own way, thus equalizing a variety of pressures every single day. The same could be said of every kind of living organism and, in fact, every kind of phenomenon in nature.)

If it's not immediately clear how every human body is always and only equalizing pressures, again, consider the pressure we feel from the anxiety that is inherent in just surviving day by day.

Take a breath.

Relax and let your body have its turn at the podium. It's always working to equalize a primal pressure to stay alive against, to put it mildly, strong odds.

Meanwhile all the other pressures are continually reasserting themselves, taking different forms, interacting in new patterns and rhythms in each moment. Many of them never do get completely equalized, at least until we die. (What might happen beyond that event is outside the scope of this book.)

Every body is always and only equalizing pressures. Equalization of pressures is one comprehensive way to view and name the innate activity of human bodies. It might work to say that it is the "raincoat" each of these human "factories" is making all the time.

Looked at from a functional perspective, this understanding may seem mechanistic, reducing human beings to nothing more sublime than a bunch of pressure-sensitive moving parts. But, looking a little deeper, I think it actually ennobles our perception of our fellow humans and ourselves.

The uncommon compassion this understanding may awaken. Indeed, this view of what we human body-persons are doing here on Earth can open us to a unique, curiously dispassionate compassion. I say "curiously dispassionate" because the view in itself is not very tender or sensitive. It *is* almost mechanistic. Instead of moving us to cherish the individual feelings, motivations, experiences, and activities of anyone or any group of our fellow humans – including, of course, ourselves – it sees all those phenomena like waves in a physicist's ripple tank, or particles in a nuclear accelerator. And it simply notices that every human body is continually struggling to equalize pressures.

The young athlete striving for victory is under an enormous internal and perhaps social pressure that only victory or a best possible performance can relieve – and then only briefly. The old man, bent by age and slowed by arthritis, looks to accommodate the pressure of surviving under conditions of increasing stiffness and pain. The growing child is adapting to living with all kinds of intense and rapidly changing influences, both from within and from without. So is the pregnant woman.

In his efforts to bring a crop to harvest and make a good sale, the farmer is continually registering and accommodating pressures from the weather, from hungry wild creatures, from creditors, from employees, and from machinery. The military man is dealing with pressures from his superiors, from subordinates, from his own simultaneous desire to fight and his fear of dying or of getting injured, and, of course, from his real or imagined enemies.

The altruistic seeker of justice struggles heroically against forces of prejudice, oppression, tyranny, exploitation. But the tyrant, the racist, the exploiter, the oppressor also has very good reasons for doing what he or she does. Selfish people, even evil ones, are under no less pressure and are no less given over to equalizing it than their opponents or detractors, however those others may judge their behavior.

A beautiful model copes with fierce pressures, internal and external, to keep her body and face just perfect. Many other women suffer equally severe pressures to make their bodies look and feel in ways that, in fact, those bodies can't.

Then there are those whose pressures are much more primal and acute. Those who are literally imprisoned. Those who have no way of knowing where they will find shelter – if anywhere. Those who don't even know if they will find enough food to eat today. Those who are at this moment realizing they are about to die – whether from illness, starvation, attack by other humans, by animals, by forces of nature that are overwhelming them right now. Those who, as I write and now as you read or listen, are actually dying, in this very moment.

And those who are at this very moment being born.

Every body is always and only equalizing pressures.

Journaling exercise for Secret #6: Make a list of the pressures you equalized yesterday. If it gets too detailed, just choose a finite period within the day. Include occasional notes or comments you find useful to write down.

You could organize this list chronologically.

You could also just take a single minute and see how many pressures you can identify that you either equalized or were in the process of equalizing at that time.

Or, to focus on another approach, you could list the pressures you equalized yesterday by category: relational, physical, energetic, emotional, psychic, mental, spiritual.

Another way to sort them is according to voluntary and involuntary activities that equalized different pressures.

Whatever way you're most inclined to go about this will be fine. Even doing a little of it could be illuminating and even provocative.

Equalizing pressures as a spiritual search. If you took a few minutes to catalog one day's equalization of pressures, or even one minute's, it is fairly self-evident that every minute and every day is its own particular version of the same basic event.

Do you get what I'm pointing to here? At the risk of over-repetition: *Every body is always and only equalizing pressures.*

Those who consider themselves spiritual seekers, for another example, suffer the limits of being mortal, vulnerable bodies. They seek to equalize those pressures by finding spiritual limitlessness. But if we can define all pressures as limiting forces, then we can also consider any attempt to equalize pressures as, on one level, an effort to achieve freedom from those limiting forces – in other words, to achieve one or another kind, quality, or form of limitlessness. Or, at least, to experience much less confining limits.

We could say, then, that, since every body is always and only equalizing pressures, every body is indeed a spiritual seeker.

Whether any specific person would think of himself as such
or not!

Is samadhi more altruistic, heroic, and true than suicide?
One of the principal ancient words for spiritual freedom and
bliss is the Sanskrit word, "samadhi" (pronounced "suh-MAH-
dhee"). And one of its root meanings is "a condition of equalized
pressures."

You might know of a person who has achieved a permanent
state of spiritual limitlessness – a kind of samadhi. This person
might have entered that state so profoundly that she says things
like, "I am not the body. I am not the mind. I am not any of these
apparent, limited things. I am really only the invisible, limitless
spirit." And she means all this with utmost sincerity. She knows
them to be her realities.

I am aware that many readers may never have heard of
such a thing. Well, it does occur. In certain, especially Oriental
or Orientally-based circles, a person's realization of this kind
of state has long been viewed as evidence of supreme spiritual
achievement. (Though they're often expected not to say so: "Those
who know, don't speak.")

It might be said that such a spiritual release from the
pressures of being here alive in and as a human body is another
form of suicide. From that perspective, suicide and samadhi are
both last-resort, ultimate efforts to equalize the pressures of living
in an absolute, conclusive way.

Is the one more altruistic, heroic, and true than the other?

I think this question has more merit than many seekers
and finders of world-transcending, body-negating samadhi
might admit.

Such a spiritual state tends to validate itself on its own
terms. In other words, in my experience, it's very difficult to
convince someone in this kind of transcendental state that they

might be leaving out a big part of their own real equation – and a much more complete and true equalization of pressures.

Yet, if you think about it, there is something inherently bizarre about hearing a human body say aloud, physically, "I am not the body." Some would say, well, that statement, when true of the person's subjective condition, points to ultimate transcendence, freedom not only from the body but from the world. And they would suggest that only this transcendence is true freedom, limitlessness, true healing of whatever is the disease that humans suffer so in this world.

I disagree. The best way I know to speak about these things is to continue to introduce what I call the body's own logic. Which leads us, in a few moments, to Secret #7.

What such world-transcenders are really looking to escape is being human *bodies*. But this is where the topic of Secret #7, the body's own logic, opens us into another realm of potential freedom, healing, wholeness, and wellness – as well as even greater relief. This is so even while the pressures of being alive continue to arise to be equalized, every moment of every day, until we die . . . and perhaps even beyond death.

First, though, let's finish with Secret #6.

Conclusion – the great relief we can find in Secret #6, including a final exercise. At every level or in every dimension of its presence and activity, every body is always and only equalizing pressures. And every kind of human being is doing his or her version of that same thing. Even those seeking to transcend being human beings!

Final exercise for Secret #6. Get up from your reading and listening and observe yourself and our human brothers and sisters. Go out into a town, turn on the TV, go online, or read a paper – do something that will expose you to human beings doing what we all keep on doing here in this world.

Feel into what makes people tick.

Of course, do this in a discreet way. Don't intrude on people's privacy or become a voyeur! It doesn't take much exposure to get a sense of what's going on with people. How a man looks at his watch while waiting for a bus can tell you volumes.

See if you can identify what general kind of pressure each person is responding or reacting to with her specific actions or non-actions.

Study at least half a dozen to a dozen people this way. Observe very different people, including some who you otherwise wouldn't pay much attention to and even may not like or be inclined to respect.

Do this exercise enough so you start to get a sense of each one's natural, instinctual, almost helpless rhythm of equalizing pressures, moment to moment, day in and day out.

In other words, find out just what kind of pressure-equalization factory each body is being from day to day.

Then, when you've observed a number of people this way to your own satisfaction, sit down somewhere quiet and peaceful and see how you feel.

My bet is, you are going to feel some serious relief indeed! And it's probably better that I not try here to say anything about what that might feel like for you.

Other than to urge you to notice that this great relief itself is evidence of . . . that's right, an equalization of a pressure in yourself. But this is one you might not have known was there until now, when it's either gone or much diminished and the contrast is so stark.

In terms of putting words on it, it's best for you yourself to feel and know what this quality of great relief is, *for you*. You've earned it.

Way back at the beginning of our discussion of this secret, I did not complete the analogy of the factory. I described my dad's factories as places dedicated to making raincoats for sale. I then described every body as a kind of factory that is dedicated to equalizing all kinds of pressures. But . . . for what? Garment factories make raincoats *for sale*. "Every Body Is Always and Only Equalizing Pressures . . . *for What?*" To what end? What's the point?

Secret #7, and the other secrets that follow, will allow us to pose answers to these questions from this new perspective that may now be emerging in you – the perspective of your *body*.

If you want an end to war, end the unconscious violence at the core of your own heart.

And if you want harmony among all peoples and nations, learn and practice the delicate dynamics of trust with every body.

If you want peace on Earth, whatever other good and righteous acts you do to help it come to pass, make those two your top priorities.

If you don't, all those other good and righteous acts remain superficial and, at last, ineffectual. They're window dressing, cosmetic changes. They can't and don't get at the heart of our species-wide crisis.

                  – Saniel Bonder, *The Tantra of Trust*

SECRET #7

The Body's Own Logic Blows Its Mind, Heals Its Heart, and Empowers Both Trust and Peace

I said something at the end of Secret #5 that I want to come back to:

"In working with people, I've observed that the mind does not have to understand this kind and depth of communication in order for the feeling heart and body to register its basic truth."

Sooner or later, yes, for the meanings to be integrated, the thinking mind must understand this or any communication. But what I am conveying here is an intelligence that pertains or belongs to the body. It is organismic logic. I am attempting to give voice to truths that – so to speak – communicate directly from and to the mind of the body itself.

The mind of the body. This mind exists in latent form in each of us. Like an underground stream, it flows on underneath our obvious currents of thinking, analyzing, interpreting, and making choices all day long. It may be underneath even the less-than-fully-conscious aspects of the mind that psychologists label "the subconscious" and "the unconscious." I'll leave it to others to try to correlate all the labels. I'm concerned here just to give voice to what I have been observing for many years about the organismic mind, the logic of our bodies.

I have been told that science has now discovered brain-
type cells in other parts of the body. The primary other location,
I'm told, is the heart; and second to that, the solar plexus. Not
surprising. Whether or not more can be made of this scientific
rumor – which is all it is for me at the moment – I do feel the
organismic logic of the body belongs principally to those other
body parts, not the brain. And, in terms of how it functions and
its basic wisdom, this organismic mind is apples to the oranges of
the brain-mind based in the center of the cranium. I sense it's even
fundamentally different from the reptilian, primitive features of
that mind based in the brain stem at the rear bottom of the skull.

The body, for instance, doesn't have to be told it is going
to die. The body doesn't need to be informed that it is always
in primal distress, even while experiencing great pleasure, joy,
or peace. The body doesn't need to be convinced that it is as
inherently sacred or, to use secular language, as fundamentally OK
as any other feature of our total nature.

That's not to say that the body can't handle some
acknowledgment. A little credit where credit is due, hm? The
body – each body – can definitely benefit by having these truths
of its own nature admitted by the more psychic parts of our being.
These parts include the thinking brain-mind, the feeling and
imaging psyche, and the deeper core of soul-nature and living
awareness.

Here is an example of the mind of the body in action. If
you are feeling in any way freed up as you read or listen to this
book, that feeling is not really psychic, or mental-emotional, in
origin. It is probably physical. You are most likely sensing relief
because the body that you are, your organismic, sensate nature, is
being seen, heard, felt, acknowledged, and addressed by what you
are reading or hearing, perhaps as never before. The body that you
are is being honored to an uncommon degree, maybe more than
ever before in your life.

Exercise and journaling for Secret #7: Ask the mind of your body to speak to you, and then just sit back and listen to what it has to say.

You may be squirming with concern that you don't know how to access the wisdom of this "mind of the body itself." You may feel cut off from it and not know how to connect with it.

The following exercise is simple, but you may have to suspend a bit of disbelief for it to work.

Here's what you can do:

- Sit in a quiet place where you will not be witnessed, overheard, or in any way disturbed.
- Take a few breaths.
- Then begin speaking to your body as if it were a separate or distinct personality.
- Address your body respectfully. Ask it for permission to be spoken to. Tell it you would like to hear from it. If you need to, feel free to say how uncomfortable or even weird you feel doing this exercise. Your body is not going to have a hard time with such feelings. It has always been covering for your attempts to keep everything together, anyway! It's always been feeling the harder feelings to accept and deal with. It's always "got your back."
- Then ask your body to tell you how it feels for it to be alive and dying. And just ask it to tell you whatever it has to say, to you personally, that will make its own life easier and bring it into greater integration with the rest of your life and mind.

You may be surprised at what the body has to say. If it will help, you can tape record your conversation with it or take notes afterward in your journal. During the conversation, it's good not to have to worry about keeping track or doing anything that will distract you from simple participation in the exercise.

Some qualities of the body's organismic intelligence.
Some of the movements of your body's "thought process" may at
first be difficult to follow. This quirky, sensate mind of each body
is not less intelligent for being so instinctual. Like a shy debutante,
it needs to be invoked and celebrated to feel free to shine. It needs
its own room and time under welcoming lights so it can truly
display its beauty and its virtues.

For instance, when I first started writing this book, I was
not at liberty to impose a mental superstructure on its unfolding.
It's not that some outside law was preventing me; rather, an
internal and inarticulate impulse needed to be given voice. I
wasn't free even to impose on it what my thinking mind might
have imagined, based on my personal experience, to be the most
crystalline logic of my own body. I had to sit down and let the
chapters just come out as they would, without apparent rhyme
or reason.

Later I began to feel at liberty to shape and reorganize
things. This was necessary to ensure that we – my body's mind and
my brain-mind both, so to speak – would be wisely taking into
account both kinds of mind in "our" readers.

But I wasn't free to come up with an outline from the
get-go. Until I got the feeling that it was time to start shaping
what had already emerged apparently at random, I had to let the
organismic intelligence have its word and its way.

Organismic logic goes in circles and spirals. It dips and darts
and flies and then hovers, and then does the same things again,
like a hummingbird. The fastest way for it to clarify things for
itself might appear, to the mind of typical thinking, to be rather
meandering and slow. Like a turtle, or a snail.

The body's own logic is like an underground stream. It's
always flowing, tumbling, streaming along. Once you start to dip
into it, you will learn how to do so at will, more or less. And this
knowing will help you conduct your life in a manner that keeps
you attuned to the body's own needs and real concerns.

One of my woman friends simply asks her body what it has to tell her. She gets a lot of messages about slowing down, not overextending herself, allowing the little things in life to take their rightful, perhaps even very big, places in her order of priorities.

Some people are not ready to allow such apparent chaos on their path of healing and growth. For some people, this kind of approach doesn't work. They may require more brain-based, conceptual structure – more of a mental framework for both their consideration and their effective, responsive action.

For another woman named Ruth, a therapist in her early sixties, this became, eventually, an agonizing dilemma. There was a deep mutual appreciation and love between us. She was quite active with others in my spiritual gatherings for nearly two years. But after a time she began to feel that she needed more of a structure than our work itself then provided.

Really, the whole process of my teaching was then at a stage analogous to the original writing of this book. Though it all made coherent sense to me, some people sometimes felt it was all chaotic and seemingly random. They wanted to be told, this is the meditation you do at this stage, and now you do these exercises, and then you will be ready for that self-observation practice, and so on.

But I couldn't present such a system. The work needed to self-reveal principally according to the logic of the body, and only secondarily then according to the systematizing logic of the mind.

This organic process needed to show its own true form. Even now, that form requires open-ended self-discovery by each individual within very general parameters. Those parameters are like guard rails on opposite sides of a road the width of a football field! They leave enormous room for groping, confusion, and self-discovery; for apparently going in circles; for not having the feeling that you are getting anywhere, not having the consolation that sure enough you are ponying up just the right experiences.

In contrast, Ruth needed an approach that could outline for her, in detail, exactly what she should do at each step of her work to deal with her issues and integrate the various parts of her nature.

I had to tell her that the particular healing and awakening process I was offering her could reveal its precise outline, steps, and details only in a unique way in each body. When that is happening, the path shows itself to be as distinctive as a thumbprint for each person. It's very concrete; there's nothing abstract or vague about it.

However, no one, myself included, can superimpose a conceptual superstructure on how this will unfold for anyone. We can say certain generic things. That, among other things, is what I am doing in this and my other books. But healing an unconscious relationship to the core wound requires each one of us to welcome, listen to, and integrate our organismic logic.

Not everybody can respond to such an apparently structure-less orientation. Ruth couldn't, and eventually, with sadness and mutual respect, we had to part company. I was powerless to provide her what she needed – at that time, anyway.

Since then my colleagues and I have been able to integrate a well-developed approach to accessing organismic logic with more structured formats, including "Great Relief Workshops" based on this book.

The body's own logic blows its mind, heals its heart, and empowers both trust and peace. All this may sound simple and even playful enough. But when you get into some of the pressurized zones of the body's logic, it can get challenging. When you encounter some of the body's real processes for dealing with long-stored trauma and distress, this logic can wreak havoc on your previous visions, beliefs, and plans about who you are and how you are going to live.

On the other end of the spectrum from those pressurized personal trauma zones, the body will never agree with Oriental philosophies that propose it is "unreal." And it will make a very strong argument to you that its own pleasures are not merely non-spiritual self-indulgences.

If you learn how to listen to this organismic stream of the body's own intelligence, your hearing and understanding will often reduce you to rapture, ecstasy, sensual pleasure and delight. One might even say "seduce" rather than "reduce." And perhaps that word "blow" can be understood to have a legitimately sexual connotation, too; I'm definitely ok with that interpretation of this secret! When you overturn the hyper-logical applecart of your brain-based, supposedly rational head-mind, you don't just plunge into dark shadow traumas of the deep psyche. You also descend into sense-based, nerve-end deliciousness.

That bodily deliciousness is one of the gateways to outgrowing our relatively unconscious relationship to the core wound. Quoting one of my other books (see p. 84), it's one of the keys to "ending the unconscious violence at the core of our own hearts" and truly practicing "the delicate dynamics of trust with every body." Trust starts at home, here in our own skin. Bizarre as it may sound, when we allow our bodies' own logic to blow our minds as I'm describing here, we become more capable of trusting ourselves and sustaining trust with others. In this way we lay real foundations for lasting peace on Earth.

Every body has innate faith. I have made many references in this book to spiritual ideas, assumptions, and practices, not so many to religious beliefs and faith. But, in the same way we can say, as I did in Secret #4, that "every body is a spiritual seeker," I believe we can also affirm that "every body has innate faith." And this is the place to say that.

Just as it has no question about whether it is going to die, the body also has no question about whether it is related to a greater Mystery, Principle, or Reality of Being. Our minds and souls, the psychic principles in our lives, can get caught up in doubts of the existence of an ultimate, all-encompassing Reality. But our bodies don't need to have any name for that Reality, nor any belief in it, in order to live continuously with perfect faith in its existence. They have neither the luxury nor the tragedy of apparent separation from That.

So the mind of the body, its organismic logic, doesn't really have room for "doubt of God" and such other fanciful notions of the poor brain-based mind. The mind of the body abides in continuous communion with the living spirit of Being, the great power that has mysteriously brought it to life, and which continually beats its heart, draws and releases every breath, and accomplishes the staggering collection of miracles necessary for every single instant of our bodily aliveness.

Does this appear to starkly contradict everything I said about our bodies' homelessness and how every body is a seeker of spirit?

I'm reminded of the poet Whitman: "Very well then, I contradict myself!"

From time to time in this book I've pointed to the stunning "both/and-ness" of the world of living paradox. This is a big both/and. Yes, that is correct: I am saying that every body is homeless here and longing for its ultimate spiritual limitlessness *and* that every body is rooted in unshakable, faithful dependence upon the spirit of Being that lives it and breathes it. Both/and.

Find out for yourself over time. See if it ain't so.

I'm suddenly inspired not to try to say much more about this. But here's a plan:

Exercise and journaling #2 for Secret #7: Once again, ask the mind of your body to speak to you, and then just sit back and listen to what it has to say.

Go back and re-read the exercise and journaling recommendations on p. 87. Do this exercise and writing again, this time especially welcoming your body to tell you whatever it has to say with respect to the matters I've brought up in these last several pages.

Conclusion – the great relief we can find in Secret #7.
I initially thought that Secret #7 would be simpler and easier for most people to get than some of the earlier ones. I expect your whole being is working on overdrive to metabolize your reactions and integrate your responses. My sense of the book's rhythm was that we needed to take a little break here.

Yet the point of Secret #7 may also be something you'll chew on for awhile . . . even the rest of your life. "The body's own logic blows its mind, heals its heart, and empowers both trust and peace."

For starters, if you can even accept this might be true, then whether or not anything of the sort has taken place for you, you can begin to exhale at a whole other depth. You can begin to sense that something of this kind is on the way for you. And that it's a good thing, fundamentally.

That "mind-blowing" organismic logic has revelations in store that are going to make your life more liveable, pleasurable, sane, and truly peaceful – even if it also intensifies challenges you already have and brings on others you can't yet anticipate.

The relief here? Just beginning to contemplate the possibility that you are now starting to integrate a whole dimension of yourself that you didn't really know was there. Giving yourself room for your body to be ok, to have its own wisdom, and for you to be able to access that from now on with increasing clarity and freedom. And deliciousness. And trust. And peace. And faith!

This can be very good news.

However, you might be feeling that you're missing the point. You might have the uneasy sense that what I am saying is going over – or under! – your head.

Not a problem, really. Here's a plan: Give yourself an opportunity to allow the body's sensate logic to release your head from its fretting and your heart from any concerns.

That suggestion might make things worse. Are you

wondering, "And just *how* am I supposed to do *that?*"

Well, I've got an incredibly cruel and difficult discipline in store for you:

Go do something fun, distracting, or pleasurable. Something way more juicy and yummy than just "taking a breath!"

Emergency Exercise for Secret #7: Let me interrupt this conclusion to emphasize that recommendation:

Really, do it:
Go have fun!
Do something playful, juicy, delicious, super-pleasurable, mindless. Do whatever gives you the most guaranteed and intense delight you can get away with legally and without risking self-destruction or endangerment of others (if you have an addiction, ahem, not that, *hm?).*

And don't even *think about* making journal entries unless that too becomes extremely pleasurable for you.

Yes, I know that if you are a longtime discipliner (read: suppressor) of pleasure, the prospect of this second exercise might strike fear in your core. You may well worry that doing this will derail a long-cultivated restraint from the material or bodily delights that would supposedly undermine your spirit's wellness and "purity."

Well, do it anyway!

If you can.

If you can't, so be it. In any case, give yourself as much of a break as possible.

Then come back later to finish this chapter and go on to Secret #8.

I mean it! Close the book. Turn off the tape. *Take the break!*

Conclusion to the conclusion. See if this isn't true: By indulging in good old-fashioned pleasure, maybe even something at least a little "forbidden," you will be far better equipped to actually encounter that next chapter's propositions, which some people would find self-indulgent in the worst way, even shockingly anti-spiritual.

First the body's own logic blows its thinking, head-based mind. It upsets its applecart, turns it upside down, makes it feel mute and stupid, pokes fun at it, strips away its cherished criteria for righteously, pompously figuring out the rights and wrongs, goods and bads, darks and lights of life.

Then, gradually, the body's own logic changes that mind and becomes a dynamic, primary part of it. Along the way, all the age-old, mumbo-jumbo dualities about "spirit" and "matter" begin resolving themselves into a marvelous new unity. You start participating consciously in life as a paradoxical dance among apparent opposites that have a singular source, foundation, and ground.

Whether or not you ever once sit down to meditate, you become a man or woman of spirit. Whether or not you can give voice to a single religious belief, you become a woman or a man of faith.

In saying this, I am projecting ahead to the largest, most dramatic forms of great relief that you may find through this book's explorations and wherever your life leads you afterward. They may await you way down long roads from where and who you are now. And that is fine. It's important now and again to indicate what's possible.

However, in doing so I don't want to burden you with a feeling that you are supposed to make any particular shift happen. I invite you to enjoy whatever kinds of great relief become natural for you as we go forward.

Secret #8 should take you at least a few steps further. Here is where, at last, we venture a definition of just what the core wound of your life actually is.

SECRET #8

Obvious Body Limits +
The Feeling, "This Is Not Enough" =
The Core Wound

The heart of the mystery that is the core wound, as best I can articulate it, is this:

We are always, inherently aware that we are limited, finite, mortal. Yet we are also always, inherently aware that there must be more to us, to life, to existence itself, than what we already know, and have, and are.

We sense or feel, even if only in a subliminal way, that we must be capable of knowing, or having, or being something limitless, infinite, even immortal. Or, if not something limitless, then something far less limited than what we are now knowing, having, or being.

This contradiction between the obvious limits we confront at all times and the impulse to know or get or be something limitless, or far less limited, triggers a perpetual conflict at the core of our lives.

In most cases we don't personally experience it as a conflict or dilemma that we can think about and name as such. Rather, we feel it more like a wound, an inexplicable, almost unnameable, pain. We endure it as something like a gash in the most intimate, private, core tissue of our very being.

Our limits are all associated with having or being a finite body. (Mind and emotions are as anchored to the body as leaves to a tree.) But if we were content, truly OK with these limits, then we would be at peace or at home in life as it already is. Our impulse toward the limitless continually translates as the feeling, "This is not enough." The helpless, perpetual mix of obvious limits and the impulse toward limitlessness makes for living as this core wound.

Obvious body limits + the feeling, "this is not enough" = the core wound. The core wound is not happening *to* us. It's not something we are experiencing. It is what we *are*. It is essential, most fundamental, existential pain. Its suffering and confusion permeate and pervade our whole lives from the very root, source, or core of our being.

The core wound is the engine of human evolution. It appears to me that, uniquely among living creatures, human beings suffer this wound, conflict, or contradiction. As a species, it makes it impossible for us to stay still. And it makes it extremely difficult for us to ever know who we really are.

Some people appear to know who they are, and so do some cultures or groups of people – at least, moreso than others. So they *appear*. Yet as a species, we stand out among cats, dogs, ants, trees, amoebae, hawks, and whales in giving chronic evidence of not knowing and being at peace with who and what we are.

If we compare the evolutionary journey of humanity with that of other creatures, something else also stands out. More than any other species', our tour of habitation on Earth has been characterized by breathtaking, accelerating rates of cultural and even in some ways physiological change.

I suggest this grand whirlwind of rapid change in human prehistory and history has been driven by one thing alone.

It's not our tool-making capability or our opposable thumbs.

It's not our endowment with a soul, a mind, or a conscience.

No, what has always driven us and continues to drive us is

our experience of this wound springing from the core of our hearts and pervading our entire lives.

It's this conflict in us between obvious limits and the impulse to limitlessness, or at least less-limitedness, of some or many kinds.

Obvious body limits + the feeling, "this is not enough" = the core wound.

Even those who appear content secretly suffer the core wound. Most human individuals don't seem to be driven by this interior conflict. Most people appear content with very few things – food, shelter, health for themselves and their families, long life, and protection from harm.

But even they secretly suffer how hard it is to be here. Even if they deny it, at a deeper level they struggle with the reality that they are dying and will lose everything they have.

And they most often give obvious evidence of that terrible struggle when they do lose the things they've been content with, and when they or others close to them die.

Just to be here, somehow sensing a potential limitlessness, freedom, and peace, or at least much greater potential fulfillment, while enduring so many limits that seem to deny us these things, is always to suffer a fundamental wound at the heart of our being.

I suggest that everything every human being has ever done – short of healing the basic, most distressing, least conscious aspects of that wound, which I'll talk about more as we continue – has been a reaction to that wound itself. It's like an itch we can never really scratch, but can't help trying to, all the time.

Of course, the core wound is also so much more than an itch. There's nothing superficial about it. Everybody suffers it. Every *body*. And every body is suffering *as* this existential wound. Do you see why I call it "existential"? It is not happening *to* us. It is not something we are *experiencing*. It *is* what we *are being*. It's innate to our being, our existence.

For the would-be suicide, like Matt, only death can promise any authentic relief from the pain of this wound. But all it can do is promise.

For the alcoholic or the addict, only mad abandonment to one's substance or behavior of choice can provide sufficient anesthesia. Yet the numbness always wears off, whereas the sting of the wound does not.

For the spiritual seeker, only more and more exalted experiences of presence, light, and bliss, or realizations of uncontained awareness, will do. But *do* they?

For the person of wealth and power, only acquiring more or holding what he has might allay the fear and anxiety. It also might not.

For the mother, only the health and well-being of the child; for the lover, only the embrace and fidelity of the beloved; for the explorer, only the finding of new horizons, the making of new discoveries; for the scientist or the scholar, only the crystallizing of new understanding and the securing of reputation.

The list goes on and on for us – we are creatures of such diverse occupations and concerns.

Yet, in truth, none of our occupations, none of our concerns, none of our confident knowings of who we are, none of our daring reaches to become and be more, ever do really suffice. The pain, confusion, anguish, and suffering of the core wound eventually percolate up through all the foundations we lay in our lives. To our great dismay, no achieved goal or state ever can finally relieve us of this distress.

How is all this sitting in you? Is it making sense? Whenever I talk about the core wound, I always feel the inadequacy of any words to do it justice.

This might be a good moment to take another breath, even a long breather. And to do an exercise.

Exercise for Secret #8: How do *you* register the core wound? Every body registers the presence and pressure of the core wound in his, her, its unique ways. You may benefit from putting down the book or turning off the tape for awhile.

Stand up, go outside, take a walk, take some deep breaths. Then contemplate these questions:

- How do you characteristically identify yourself? (Examples would be some of the types of people I listed above, or "musician," "sister," "veterinarian," "poet," "just an ordinary guy," and so on. Most of us have several primary forms of self-identity, not just one.)
- How, as the person you are, do you most commonly register the core wound between your obvious body limits and the feeling, "this is not enough"?
- What primal emotions or states of mind come with that feeling? (Examples: frustration, hopelessness, anger, sadness, self-pity, worthlessness, fear, confusion, feeling of being cut off or alienated, and so on.)
- How have you coped with that core wound and those primal emotions or states of mind all your life till now?
- Can you detect any patterns in your coping or your reactions to the wound and the feelings/states of mind that attend it?

Journaling for Secret #8. Record anything you like that has come up during your reading and the exercise. Include any questions or confusion you may have about what the core wound actually is – for you personally, and also for all of us in general.

Conclusion – the great relief we can find in Secret #8. Let me move toward closing this chapter with a summary statement that also goes a little further.

The central mystery of our existence is what I call the core wound. It appears to me that, among living creatures, the core wound is unique to human beings.

We can define it as this predicament: We know we are limited, finite, and mortal in our bodily lives. Yet we forever sense, intuit, or at least hope that we might become limitless, infinite, and immortal, here or elsewhere – somehow free of death and all, or at least many, of the pains of our obvious limits. All the kinds of seeking and striving that human beings have done historically can be understood as a helpless, unending, relatively unconscious reaction to this wound.

Obvious body limits + the feeling, "this is not enough" = the core wound.

The last thing I'll say here is that, yes, our experience of the core wound can change, even dramatically. Because the core wound is not just happening to us, but is what we *are*, the core wound itself cannot be healed. But our reactive, unconscious relationships to its presence at the heart of our lives can indeed be healed. And this can provide truly great relief for the rest of our lives.

Even so, I expect that the reality of life after this basic healing will never be what any individual expects beforehand. And the quality of existence as a wound, an unnameable gash somehow at the heart of our being and simultaneously pervading our whole lives, does not disappear in that healing. It simply becomes increasingly *conscious*. I'll explain why and how this is so as we continue.

The relief to be found here? Whew.

There's a scene in the movie *Dances with Wolves* where the Native American man played by Graham Greene says to the Kevin Costner character something like, "You're a real human being!" He's surprised because he's never before encountered anything like sane, simple humanness in a paleface.

Getting the ungive-back-able, untranscendable, inescapable, plain old "comes-with-the-human-turf" *givenness* of the core wound to any degree and at any level begins to poke a hole in a great big dam in our hearts. Even any trickle of the pent-up, stifled, bewildered energy of life that starts flowing out that hole, however tiny, begins to liberate us into our lives as never before.

It starts to dawn on us that maybe, finally, we are becoming real human beings.

Since words cannot come close to doing justice to these matters, you may be feeling confused right now. That's OK. In the kind of work that you and I are doing together, confusion is the first sign of a new understanding emerging. In other words, it's a good sign. It signals that a shift is taking place underneath the rational mind, one that will articulate itself there in your thinking later.

Please take a breath or two.

Allow whatever feelings you are having, whatever reactions or responses are coming up, to just go ahead and be there.

I am well aware that you may need to discover more about this whole secret for it to crystallize as your own innate understanding.

In fact, reading this book is just a start on that journey, or a next step. Your whole being will go through shifts and changes that reveal this holistic understanding – and, truly, great relief! – over time.

One of the inadequacies of words is that we can only say
one of them at a time. Our experience of life, meanwhile, is always
multidimensional and simultaneous. So much is always going
on at once, and on so many levels! Please bear with me, then, as
I keep trying to drape a few more linear strings of helpful words
through the forests of our omnidirectional, continuous experience.
Let's go on to Secret #9.

SECRET #9

You Can't Heal the Core Wound, But You Can Gradually Become Conscious Of It, In It, and As It

I've been whispering this essential secret to you all along our way together, starting with a gentle suggestion in Secret #1.

Having now tried there in Secret #8 to summarize what the core wound is, here as this book comes to a close it's time to shout this summary secret itself from the rooftops.

Or better yet: Let me ask you to just say it aloud yourself a few times, with intense concentration.

And let's treat these verbal repetitions as if the words' meanings were heavy physical objects. Why not bring your whole body into this exercise? In this weightlifting of meanings, the following exercise is a way for you to let yourself feel the significance of every word to the fullest.

In fact, if we were in a gym, and if what I will soon invite you to say out loud were packed onto a barbell, it would be one of the heaviest weights you have ever tried to lift.

As in strength training, a few good reps will make you feel a lot stronger pretty quickly. Especially if you take it real slow and smooth. In super-slow weightlifting, nearly every muscle and fiber of your body gets to participate in the lift, and the relaxation is in its own way equally intense.

Exercise for Secret #9: Heavy Lifting. Lie down on your back somewhere. A bench would be nice, but it's not necessary. Just make sure your arms are relatively free to move.

Then imagine you are holding a barbell with massive weights just above your chest. It might be the heaviest weight you ever attempted to lift. You are going to do three extremely slow repetitions of raising and lowering it.

Let each press upward and each relaxation back down take ten seconds or so. On each movement, say Statement #1 or Statement #2, as indicated here, aloud, slowly, one word at a time, with concentration. Make the raising and lowering real; clench your muscles and concentrate as if you were dealing with an immense weight that could hurt you if you didn't do the exercise correctly.

You may not understand the meanings of what I will ask you to say. You also may not agree. Still, as in Secret #5, please be willing on a provisional, temporary basis to try this exercise on for size. At least until you finish reading or listening to this book, be willing to grant that these statements may be true for you.

Actually doing the exercise while holding open that possibility might just help the meanings sink in for you.

(For maximum effect, you can do this with a real barbell or dumbbells. If you do, please don't try to lift a challenging amount of weight. An amount that's enough to really feel, but still within your easy capacity, is a much better idea. You want to focus on the meaning of what you are saying, not on the physical activity.)

Ready? Here we go:

As you press up, slowly say Statement #1 out loud:

"I . . . Can't . . . Heal . . . My . . . Core . . . Wound."

As you let down, slowly say Statement #2, also out loud:

*"But . . . I . . . Can . . . Gradually . . . Become . . .
Conscious . . . Of . . . It, . . . In . . . It, . . . and . . . As . . . It."*

Press up again, speaking aloud:

"I . . . Can't . . . Heal . . . My . . . Core . . . Wound."

Let down again, saying the words clearly:

*"But . . . I . . . Can . . . Gradually . . . Become . . .
Conscious . . . Of . . . It, . . . In . . . It, . . . and . . . As . . . It."*

Don't forget to take at least ten seconds on the way up, with a slow, smooth motion all the way, and the same timing and smooth, slow motion on the way down. One last repetition:

Press up and speak:

"I . . . Can't . . . Heal . . . My . . . Core . . . Wound."

Let down and speak:

*"But . . . I . . . Can . . . Gradually . . . Become . . .
Conscious . . . Of . . . It, . . . In . . . It, . . . and . . . As . . . It."*

Thank you! Now please take a break and a breath or two – as if you had just finished an intense actual exertion and need to regain your breath.

When you've regained composure, let's resume.

Why make such a big deal of this secret? For one thing, because we all want to get rid of any pain we feel. Whether it's physical, emotional, or of any other nature, as soon as we notice pain, we want to ease it. Again, from my perspective there is nothing wrong with that instinct. It's natural.

But the core wound is a pain we cannot at last eliminate. So to make these statements aloud in this out-there way allows every part of our bodies as well as our minds to walk farther down the road toward owning the import of the words.

In the earlier years of my work I used to talk about "healing the core wound." As I contemplated our human predicament over time, however, I found it necessary to change that language. "Healing" is just not what can and does happen to the core wound in reality. The great relief occurs instead by our deeply accepting the core wound and feeling it. When we cease to react instinctively to the painful, pervasive, bewildering intensity of the core wound, we don't cure it – we fall into it and at last *become* it.

Each of the sacred secrets I've presented in this book is a gateway into that acceptance, feeling, ceasing, falling, and becoming. If you come back to this book after you finish a first reading, you might notice yet other qualities of great relief coming through for you. Altogether, this book and my whole teaching provide gradual access to the transformation of our *relationship* to the core wound. More and more, we heal ourselves of adding unconscious reactions to the abiding reality of the core wound. We don't heal the wound itself.

I said it earlier in a way that bears repeating: We cease adding unnecessary pain to inevitable pain.

The three great phases of realizing the core wound: becoming conscious "of it, in it, and as it." The word "realize" itself can have many meanings. When I speak here of the three great phases of realizing the core wound, I am using that word in the simple sense of "making real."

If you've been following the thread of this book's considerations, all along the core wound has likely been taking shape as an actuality for you. You've been making it real for yourself.

I wanted to explore some of the core wound's primal implications in our lives before venturing its definition in Secret #8. I felt it necessary to concretize some of its effects before trying to say directly what it *is*. What the core wound *is*, is innate to our subjective experience of being alive. It's not something we can experience as an objective thing of any kind, physical (like a finger) or psychic (like a thought or feeling). It's what we are *being*.

All these secrets of how the core wound's presence impacts us are like sunshine, while the core wound is more like the sun. Those qualities of its impact are objective features of being alive that we can and do experience: "It's Really Hard to Be Here," "Every Body Is Homeless Here." The core wound, however, is what the self knows itself to be as the *experiencer*. It's the essence of our subjective "I"-ness.

So I wanted you to have a chance to feel and verify for yourself some of the objective effects of the sunshine's light and heat before making anything like an abstract statement, "The core wound is 'X'," which would be like asking you to look directly at the subjective sun.

I hope exploring the first eight secrets has helped you do that. If so, then you have entered at least the first of these three phases of realizing the core wound. You have begun to become conscious "of it." And you may also have started becoming conscious "in it," and perhaps even "as it."

Yes, I know this seems to imply that the core wound is an object you are experiencing, so it sounds like I'm contradicting the whole point I was just making! Well, it's impossible to make altogether rational sense of the somewhat awkward and certainly mysterious transitions we go through in this journey.

More on the analogy of sunlight and the rising sun. Maybe
that comparison to our experience of sunshine and the sun itself
can help us more here. What happens at dawn every day is a
process in which, if we happen to be awake, at first we become
aware of the sun's presence in our lives without yet being able to
see the sun itself.

Observing myself and many others over more than a decade
now, I can see that, in general, people first become aware "of" the
core wound at the heart of our lives. But it's still somehow an "it"
to us. It's "out there," or even "inside," present but still somehow
elsewhere. We can strongly feel the reality of many or all of the
first seven secrets, for instance, and we may enjoy increasing great
relief by having understood them as parts of our real lives. But the
core wound itself is still perhaps distant, unclear, hidden
from view.

This phase of becoming conscious "of" the core wound
is analogous to how we feel when the first rays of dawning light
begin to change our perception of the world. The sun has not yet
risen, most of the world is perhaps still in deep shadow. But the
light has permeated the sky and is becoming a prominent factor in
our perception. Birds are beginning to sing their songs. There's a
general sense of a new day on the way.

After awhile, our relationship to the core wound changes.
It becomes a major part of our subjective landscape. We sense it
more and more as the context of our whole lives. At that stage
we are becoming conscious "in" the core wound. It's no longer
mostly somewhere else. It's the "here" that we are always living and
moving in. We sense it to be our truth at the core and yet we also
sense that it pervades our whole world.

This phase of becoming conscious "in" the core wound
bears similarities to how we feel when the sunshine has so fully
permeated the sky that all the living creatures wake up and
everyone feels a little heat returning to the world along with

increasing light. Now the light of the sun is no longer simply entering a dark realm. It has replaced the darkness so much that we're now aware of the light as the dominant feature of the world we live in. Often a breeze picks up at this hour.

The sun still hasn't risen. We aren't yet able to see it directly. But, whereas earlier its light was only a new kind of *content* coming into a world that was basically dark, now its light has replaced darkness as the *context* of our sense-experience of the world.

Just so, when we are initially becoming conscious "of" the core wound in our lives, it is something like a new kind of content coming into our world as it's been for so long. But when we also start becoming conscious "in" the core wound, it is replacing our previous sense of the entire context of our experience. We're no longer just aware "of" it. We're becoming aware "in" it.

Does this make sense? I realize that this whole discussion can be a bit abstract.

(If you need to, take a breath or two. When you're ready, let's keep going.)

Even so, while becoming conscious "in" the core wound we're still not entirely one with it. It's becoming the ground of our being, the context of our experience, but there's a way in which we still feel apart from it.

And then, over more time, it begins to dawn on us that we are indeed *being* the core wound ourselves. (When I first wrote that sentence, I didn't even notice I'd used the word "dawn.") The core wound becomes us; or we become the core wound. In that phase we have made it most real to ourselves. We have become conscious not just "of" and "in" the core wound. We have become conscious "as" the core wound. We know ourselves to *be* that paradox of simultaneous limits and limitlessness. We are being that principle that drives toward what might be even as it accepts what is.

This phase of becoming conscious "as" the core wound, then, is like the time when the sun is actually becoming visible over the horizon. Now we can see it directly. From this point forward both its light and its heat intensify, and the whole living world comes to greater life and activity in its radiance. Flowers turn toward it and open, creatures bask in its heat. Now we are no longer merely aware of some of the effects of the sun's light. We are perceiving it directly and indeed can look straight into it, at least momentarily.

Of course, here the analogy breaks down. When we are dealing with the deeper mysteries of life, natural comparisons almost always come up short. The sun, after all, remains an object, even if a very bright one, whereas the core wound is at the root of our subjective sense of who we are.

Exercise #2, with possible journaling, for Secret #9: Wake up before dawn tomorrow, go outside, and experience the three phases of the dawn. While you are doing so, consider and feel into this analogy of experiencing sunshine and the sun and the three phases of becoming conscious "of," "in," and "as" the core wound.

This exercise might work well enough even on a cloudy day, but sometime soon do it on a day when you actually get to see the sun itself coming over the horizon.

If it will help you at the time, you can bring the book with you. If you are reading it in print, take a flashlight with you so you can reread the preceding section on the analogy of sunlight and the rising sun. If you're listening on tape, take a portable cassette or CD player and listen to that section. And, either way, also read or listen to the next sections too, until I start speaking of something completely different.

As you experience the three phases of the dawn, feel deeply into these three phases of becoming conscious in relation to the core wound.

Afterward, it might help to record any thoughts or feelings this exercise brought up for you in your journal.

How I got really familiar with the differences among the three phases of the dawn. Speaking of the rising sun, I am an avid golfer and like to play first thing in the morning. I often arrive at my golf course just before dawn. So I've had the opportunity to discover the differences among the three phases of the dawn that I've described here.

In the first phase, yes, there's light in the sky, but for quite awhile I still can't hit a golf ball and hope to see where it went. In fact, it takes some time before I can even clearly see it on a tee in front of me! I've learned the hard way how important it is to be able to see the ball well enough. Good thing some of those misses occurred under cover of darkness!

During the second phase, in contrast, I can see quite well even though the sun itself is not yet visible. The light has made play possible. In fact, I could play a whole round in that kind of light.

However, it's not yet very warm out. Several years ago a videographer friend offered to make a short documentary on my spiritual work. She also wanted to show me in my ordinary daily life. So we agreed and got the golf club's permission that she would come out and walk around the first few holes with me and shoot some film.

I was under the impression she'd be able to start filming sometime on the first hole, if not right at the first tee, so I told her to come meet me there. But it turned out there wasn't enough light. Meantime, there also wasn't much heat, and even though it was midsummer, in the early morning air she was freezing!

Well, I was quite embarrassed at how poorly I had estimated the intensification of both the light and the temperature for her. She wasn't able to start filming – and warming up – until we got to the fourth tee about thirty minutes later. Turns out she couldn't really get a clear image or stop shivering until the full force of the risen sun had come into the landscape.

Perhaps these similarities between the three phases of sensitivity to the core wound and the phases of the sun's daily dawning may help you deepen in your appreciation of this book's sacred secrets.

Here's an important emphasis: There's no need to project off to becoming conscious "as" the core wound – the full heat and light of a risen sun – as if only then will great relief become possible for you. That may be another way this sun-and-sunlight analogy doesn't quite fit. As you may already have discovered, you can find a lot of brightness, warmth, even some real heat perhaps, all along the way of becoming conscious "of" and "in" the core wound. It's a gradual unfolding, with small or great doses of relief and ultimately happy disillusionment at every stage.

The structure of this book allows you to discover that unfolding for yourself. It's been a kind of circle or spiral, a following of the body's own apparently meandering logic, taking you to some central considerations. Even now, you may not yet be able to make much sense of what it might be to become conscious "as" the core wound, or even really "in" it. But no one can take away from you the qualities of great relief you are already enjoying while becoming conscious "of" the core wound in the ways you have. If the "in" and "as" phases are also coming to life for you, bravo; but if not, so what?

Many readers and listeners won't even want to try to figure out where they are in this sequence of three phases of great relief. The whole discussion may seem quite beside the point – which is the actual relief they're already tapping into. If that's how you feel, that's fine.

Because these three phases of the revelation of great relief do have distinctive qualities and also challenges as you go through them, it's been important to me to mention them here.

Each of this book's secrets, other things I write or say, and many resources others and I can point you to, can help you continue to cultivate this gradual transformation. You can check into the Afterword, "Where Can I Go from Here?," at the end of this book.

Yet it's also true that you may not need anything beyond this book itself, at least for now. In my own experience, each of these secrets is itself an inexhaustible mother lode of great relief. Any time I dig into any one of them even a little bit, I come up with more gems! The same could well prove true for you, and I welcome you to find out.

James and his crime. Now let's take Secret #9 a little closer to heart, and, I hope, help dispel any feeling of distress, unclarity, or inadequacy that that last whole discussion may have prompted in you, by considering something completely different.

I started this book with the story of Matt and his suicide. Let's move toward closing it with the concrete, real-life story of another man for whom it appears the core wound became tragically unbearable – at least for a time. We'll call this man James. To protect his privacy and that of others involved, I will change some details of his story, but nothing critical for what we are exploring together in this book and this secret.

Unlike Matt's, James's story is still unfolding as I write and no doubt as many of you read or listen. Just learning what has happened so far, however, will lead us into some pertinent final reflections on how we can and can't "get at" the core wound. And it will take us into a vantage point on freedom, love, and trust that will permit the book to end with yet another beginning in the ever-renewing journey of great relief.

James is a professional tradesman and business owner who lives in a small city in the Midwest. I have known him for many years, having met in the chance ways life provides. We did a little business together and made enough of a connection to stay in touch from time to time. But we were never close, never really friends; more like friendly acquaintances. Our business relationship ended quite a few years ago when he moved from where I was living. Since then, for whatever reason, we've kept in occasional touch through holiday greetings and rare phone calls just to say hello.

One of the things that plugged us in together for longer than our business connection lasted is how trustworthy James is in a field where trustability is sadly not a common customer experience. When we had frequent professional interactions, I gave him a number of referrals because I could trust that he and his group would give completely fair estimates and do very reliable work. I think those referrals and my acknowledgement of how much I trusted his work were the bonds that kept a connection going after he moved.

I was also aware all along that James is a kind of driven guy, into extreme sports and a bit hyper. I knew that he and his wife Marilyn had a couple of kids since moving. I had said hello to her once or twice in earlier years, when she was running his office.

My sense of James's edginess did not prepare me, however, to find out last year that he had been arrested for a violent crime against someone he did not even know.

It wasn't murder or rape, but it was bad – really bad. A mutual acquaintance heard the news and called to tell me about it. That person told me the news stories out where James and Marilyn lived were even broadcasting photos of his place of work and their home. Apparently he'd been completely blasted on drugs. It was so shocking. I have never known and certainly never trusted anyone who has later done something so dreadful to another human being. The only thing I heard that first night that sounded like the James I knew was that he had started apologizing immediately after his arrest.

Over the weeks that followed I got word to Marilyn that, whatever had happened, I would support James and her in any way I could. Through other avenues, I pieced together more of the story. It sounded like James was now a broken man and it was hard to imagine he could have anything but a horrific future.

Every violent crime is a perfect tragedy. Did you ever see the movie *The Perfect Storm?* If you haven't, what I want to say here won't ruin it for you. It's based on an actual event in the North Atlantic Ocean off New England, where three different intense storm systems collided to produce a mega-storm – and a searing human drama.

Over the months after learning of James's actions, it occurred to me that every crime, especially every violent crime, is a perfect tragedy.

No matter how heinous, every criminal is also a human being – and a very broken one at that. His or her actions are wild, desperate – even if calculated and deliberately evil – attempts to somehow grasp an imagined freedom from the pressurizing limits of being alive.

A violent crime like James's produces a ripple effect of dreadful karmic consequences in the lives of everyone it touches.

Here this trusted and well-respected man, a relatively young husband and father of two young children, has completely branded his victim's whole present and future with an incomprehensible violation from which that person will never fully recover. It would be hard to overestimate the personal holocaust this crime has visited upon the victim and the victim's family and friends.

He has also devastated his own entire life and also that of his wife and his children.

And then there are all the people who know James, his own family and friends, all his customers, and, in wider circles, everyone who even hears about this crime and its consequences. Every time someone does something like this it makes us all even more fearful for ourselves and our loved ones, distrustful of one another, and despairing of the very possibility for harmony, peace, and trust in our human relations.

If we understand tragedy as an event in which a lesser trait or potential brings down and destroys something far greater, not only for the protagonist but for many others around him or her, then, like that "Perfect Storm," James's crime is indeed a perfect tragedy.

"A kind of awakening." Over the months afterward I kept meaning to make a trip to where James is incarcerated to see him.

I just felt I might be able to be someone in his life who could be of some help. Through Marilyn I sent a couple of messages of Linda's and my support for them. I was hesitant to do this, but the employees at their place of business encouraged me, and Marilyn later told me she and James were very grateful.

An extremely busy travel schedule, a sudden move to a new home that Linda and I had not planned but found necessary, and other events of a busy life continued to delay my visit.

Eventually I had another conversation with Marilyn. Among other things she mentioned that James seemed to be coming out of the darkest depression and distress about what he had done and how he felt about himself as someone who could do that.

She then said, "I hope this doesn't sound weird, Saniel, but I have to say, he's going through *a kind of awakening.*" That got my attention. As little as I knew James and Marilyn, I knew they didn't commonly talk like this. "Awakenings" are central to my life and business, but not, before now, to theirs. Something unexpected and extraordinary was happening.

She explained that James was beginning to take stock of his life in ways he never had before. He was now seriously working with the therapist the county justice system was providing. And he was beginning to see that he had been destroying himself before the crime, but now, even despite all the continuing terrible consequences for his victim, himself, and their families, he was seeing that he can and must take responsibility for his life at levels he never has before.

A Sunday morning revelation. All of that, of course, was heartening to me. But when I finally was able one Sunday morning in early 2004 to go see James while giving seminars in their region of the country, I did not know what kind of shape I'd find him in. I've seen many people begin to recognize the call to take greater responsibility for their lives, only to falter and regress under the pressures they face from day to day. His pressures are obviously immense.

When I saw James, I was astonished.

His eyes were clear – far clearer than I had ever seen them before.

His complexion almost glowed.

It was as if the man had shed a skin.

He was happy to see me. When I apologized for not getting there sooner, he said it was just as well – he'd needed some hard time to go down deep into what it all really meant for him, and he had not been a sociable human being during those previous months. He was glad I had not come till now.

On my side, I had the disconcerting feeling the whole time I was there with him – probably an hour and a quarter – that I was talking with someone as conscious as the people I work with directly around the issues I've spoken of in this book. In all the years of previous association we'd never shared a word about my work and matters of the heart, soul, and spirit. But there on the other side of the reinforced plate glass, in his orange jail jumpsuit, I was encountering a man whose heart and soul had only been able to begin coming alive and awake by his first doing this dreadful thing that he will, and should, repent the rest of his days.

One of the first things James told me was that throughout his life, starting at least in high school, he had assumed that someday he would kill himself. He had not had a particularly dreadful life. He just always felt he was going to take himself out of it. Even after marrying, creating a successful business, and having children, none of that had changed.

As we talked it became clear to me that on some level he had done just that. He had arranged to go through a death while alive. Tragically, the way he did it perpetrated an atrocious crime on an innocent victim who may have a much harder time getting past the violence of what he did than he will. But unlike Matt, James did not literally take himself out of this life. And now, in jail, as a violent felon who is likely to be put away for many years, James is also going through a rebirth.

He told me details of how he had become more and more estranged and constricted within the pressures of his life and his business. He told me that now he has discovered an entirely different purpose for his life, and how much he wants to live and hopes to have another chance someday to make his life right outside prison. He said that he and Marilyn, despite the circumstances and the terrible thing he did, are closer than they've been in a long time, because he's found himself in such a whole new way.

Before the crime James was running himself into the ground, and the stress he was carrying and the ways he was abusing himself were wrecking his body and mind. No one else had known how carried away he was with the drugs. It was not a longtime habit, but once he'd gotten into it, that suicidal impulse in him started driving him closer and closer to an edge. Finally, he'd gone right over it.

Not knowing whether he was religious and I should therefore couch my comments in terms of his faith, I asked James if he had any relationship to God. He said that he respects everyone's right to whatever God they may have, but as for him – he tapped his chest at the center of his heart – what he feels like he's got to do first is just really find himself.

He said even his relationships to his children are better than they were before, as devastated and shocked as the kids can't help but be. He had been so absent and so desperately missing from his own life and from his family. He told me details of the events leading up to the crime that are not appropriate to share. But I could certainly see how the man just went over the deep end that day.

I let James know that, his terrible action notwithstanding, I know he is fundamentally a good man. I also said that due to my many years of working with people and uncovering the depths in our hearts, while I couldn't possibly condone or excuse what he did, I do not condemn him for having done it. To me, though I don't deny the existence of evil in people, James is not evil. He committed an evil action for which he will be paying a high price for a long time. But he is already paying the most important price, using everything that has happened as fuel for his own soul-searching and redemption.

I told him that morning that he is now on the path to cultivating and fulfilling the goodness in him others of us have always seen, at least in his professional service. He told me he always appreciated that I referred people to him on the basis of my trust of him. I said that now he was going to be learning more and more about himself on the deeper levels of his being so he can eventually trust himself where he has never even known himself before.

James said that he is now meditating each day. He showed me the charts and journals he keeps so that he can just live one day at a time, grow one step at a time, and keep on developing a positive presence in his own life and that of others who know him. He's learning about creative visualization and is interested in finding out more about the life of the spirit. He described how he has entered a frequent correspondence with a niece whom he'd barely known before. I was also glad to hear that his whole family has rallied around him. Most everyone who knows him sees that this was not the act of a hardened criminal but that of a desperate man. Sadly, a few friends and a few customers have fallen away, unable to see what others of us do.

James's prospects are not good. In the weird ways of our criminal justice system, his very willingness to admit and repent of his wrongdoing in the earliest moments after the crime may work to his disadvantage. At this writing his case is still in the pre-trial stage. Once in prison, which is pretty much a foregone conclusion, he may be moved at the system's whims without notice, and the only way his family and friends will find out when that happens is after he contacts them by mail. And he may well be in prison for many, many years to come, perhaps even the rest of his life.

Meanwhile Marilyn has already had to sell their house to deal with legal fees. She and the team at their business are carrying on. I have tremendous admiration for her. Who can know what she has gone through and continues to endure? She has not wavered in her commitment to James and their lives together – even though now they may be facing a terribly long time apart. There's just no way to turn this kind of tragedy into a happy ending.

Before I left the jail that Sunday morning I told James I would try to come see him as often as I can and keep up the connection from now on. I let him know that part of the way I can serve as I do is by being able to see deeply into people's souls, and that I can see he has made a tremendous change in his heart. More than that, I can see he is now embarking on a lifelong project that can make his transformation a gift to others as well.

I urged him to keep up his journaling. It can document an inner development that may someday be of help to others who are imprisoned or feel like they are, or who themselves have fallen into the depths of the human heart where he has now begun to confront his demons – and himself.

I told James he is something of a monk now. He has found a way, admittedly bizarre and tragic, to get himself confined away from the common world, where he is now actively negotiating a remarkable resurrection of his character that can't help but be a blessing for himself and others. He acknowledged the truth of that. He only hopes that someday, sooner than later, he can emerge and be with his family again, and that then he can live the kind of life of which both they and he will be proud. He also knows that might never happen. He's just taking his new life one day at a time.

Time for a major break and a whole bunch of breaths.
Please take a break now. I recommend a long one. If I have
managed to tell James's story with any transparency at all, it is
bound to have stirred up a swirl of feelings and thoughts in you. I
recommend putting the book down, or turning off the tape, for a
good long while before returning to complete it.

On your break, take a whole bunch of deep breaths. This
is a true human tale none of us will ever forget. Let's let it sink in
however it will for awhile.

More journaling for Secret #9. I could say a lot about the relevance of James's story to our own lives and these many secrets our bodies want us to know about freedom, love, trust, and the core wound of our lives. But before I offer just a few reflections that will help us crystallize Secret #9 and tie this whole book together, why don't you first reflect on James and his predicament yourself?

You may wish to respond to these questions or suggestions in your journal:

- How does James's story touch or impact you? What feelings does it bring up?
- Go back and take a few moments to explore how, in your view, James's life may exemplify each of the nine secrets covered in this book. In what ways was he suffering a lack of awareness of the reality of each secret in his life? In what ways, if any, have those situations changed for him, as best you can be aware from what I've told you?
- Have you ever felt impulses like the ones that James was suffering, and the ones he acted out? If so, describe them. If you feel hesitant to write them down even in your private journal, at least think deeply upon them. Recall the time and place they arose and what you felt tempted to do or say.
- In what ways, if any, has the great relief you've found through this book's sacred secrets helped ease, clarify, or unburden your own heart at these deeper levels of your own most antisocial or self-destructive impulses?

If James and Marilyn can do their heavy lifting, you and I can do ours. I told James's and Marilyn's story here at some length to help this point really sink in. If they can do their work to find greater freedom, love, and trust under such conditions of excruciating shock and distress, most of us can probably muster up what it takes to do our work in our own circumstances.

The pain of living is not something we can erase or destroy.

The shock of being so limited and wanting such freedom from limits is not something we ever exactly get over. Even when the day might come when we somehow access a spiritual limitlessness, the wound of "both/and" remains. The limits will still persist! Especially if we keep learning these sacred secrets our body wants us to know about these primary concerns of life, we see that the core wound always remains. It simply becomes increasingly conscious.

We can indeed become evermore aware of being at once so limited and so hungry for limitlessness, or for a much greater freedom from limits. We can become increasingly conscious of that core wound, in that core wound, and eventually, as that core wound.

How do James and his discoveries of deeper facts of life relate to this book's secrets? Without a manual, instinctively, he has made his way forward into a new life of growing sensitivity to these matters. And with it has come great relief.

Before his crime James was certainly feeling that "something was wrong, missing, or unclear at the core of his life" – and pervading it. Now he's doing the work to heal himself. In practical terms, he is addressing the extremity of that distress in his own depths in many ways. And he is also permitting himself the paradox of feeling more at home in his own skin as a self-confessed violent felon than he ever was before as a respected family man and business owner. Great relief in Secret #1.

James acknowledged not just an impulse to commit suicide someday but an assumption he would. In his own bizarre and violently criminal way, he did destroy his life as he'd known it, much of it anyway. Yet now he is alive as he never was before. Whereas before he was only reacting to it, now he comprehends in his heart that "it's really hard to be here" in this life. What he did that he can never eradicate, and the further shocks he may suffer in court, in prison, and in events in the lives of those he loves, guarantee him plenty more experience of setbacks too. Yet his acceptance of these realities is so deep it is changing him even at the material level, in his skin and physiognomy. He looks like and is a different, much happier man. Great relief in Secret #2.

James was a guy who may not have had everything but surely had a lot. None of it was "enough." None of it was IT. Now he has deprived himself of everything he cherished, at least in outward terms. Who knows how many years will pass before he gets to hug his wife and children again, if ever? It's heartbreaking. And there's no guaranteeing he won't lose the shine of his apparent transformation and sink back irretrievably into much darker places again. (I doubt it, but we will have to see.) Even so, he is well on the road to recognizing the prisons of his previous ITs and will have great resources for continuing to understand the ITs that are beckoning him forward even today. Great relief in Secret #3.

Before his crime, James was clearly one of the desperately "homeless living under an expensive roof." Now he's living in a prison cell, which will be his so-called home for years to come. But he is far more at peace than ever before with how exposed and helpless it is to be human and alive. Great relief in Secret #4.

The sheer brute force of James's anxiety prior to what he did that landed him in jail is gone now. He may not be thinking about it, but he has become intimate with just how anxious he was walking around being – just what a time bomb his heart and soul were until he exploded and went, to all appearances, completely mad. It's just beginning to dawn on him, I sense, how anxious he was at the heart – and how "every body has an anxious heart," struggling to stay alive. Great relief in Secret #5.

Here is a man who had to erupt and do one of the worst things he could possibly have done in order just to begin to ease and equalize the pressures he was under. To many an onlooker it would appear that he has inherited a life of far more intense pressures. Why is he so serene, at least for now, and so dedicated to an ongoing transformation? Great relief in Secret #6.

There is a way in which James's body claimed its own life when he was ready to throw away and destroy his mind as he had known it, his sense of self-worth and his reputation, his closeness with his family, and so much more of what we tend to require to stay sane. He didn't literally kill himself as he'd so long thought he would. He did end much of his life as he'd known it but now is finding gateways into a new one. In this one, he is listening to his body's own logic as never before. And, yes, while it is certainly blowing his previously developed mind, it is also, under the most unlikely of circumstances, healing his heart, opening him to new currents of trust both in himself and with others, and conferring peace upon a life was so deeply troubled for at least half his years that he just matter-of-factly assumed someday he would end it. Great relief in Secret #7.

Thus, while I am pretty confident he never thought about any such thing, James is well on his way to encountering the paradoxes of combining within one heart, soul, and body these contrasts: obvious body limits plus the feeling, "this is not enough!" The drama of the tension between limits he felt crushing the life out of him and a ferocious desire for limitlessness led him to break society's laws and do a terrible thing to an innocent. What he has gleaned from that plunge off the cliff of his own reason is, among other things, great relief in Secret #8. If not consciously, he has certainly begun to live it bodily.

It may take James awhile to put all of this together. He may not agree with some of my senses of where he stands with it all. But I think he has surrendered keenly into the early stages of becoming conscious both of the core wound and in it. "As" is another long leg of the journey away, perhaps, or maybe not. In any case, though he has not yet read this book and is probably not thinking in these terms, James is surely experiencing some of the great relief available in Secret #9.

Conclusion – the great relief we ourselves can find in Secret #9 and in this book altogether. Two forms of this at once exalting enrichment and humbling release come immediately to my mind to be acknowledged here:

1. Knowing that the journey of great relief is ours to make each in our own unique ways, and that it can never end, at least as long as we are alive on this Earth.
2. Knowing that even in the most wretched, humiliating, dreadful of circumstances, like James's, the journey of great relief *is still ours to make each in our own unique ways, and that it can never end, at least as long as we are alive on this Earth.*

"I can't heal my core wound, but I can gradually become conscious of it, in it, and as it." One way this insight sears through us feels like a disappointment. We were all hoping for a miracle cure, right? Sorry. And it's not just that we don't get the fairy-tale miraculous healing. We don't get a complete healing, *period.* That option is not in the terms of this deal of living.

But in another way, it's a huge gift to be released into the reality of how life actually is, and to be able therefore to own this secret personally. Once you begin to grasp it even a little bit, no one can take this secret away from you. And knowing that, in itself, turns out to be a major healing after all.

Then you can start relaxing into an ownership not just of a secret, or even a book of secrets, but of a mystery. And the more you relax into that ownership, the more it dawns on you that this whole sequence of secrets is not just *a* mystery. It is somehow also a gateway to *the* Mystery. The *Mystery,* itself.

Here I come to the place in the book where I assumed I would have some wondrous, beautiful, compelling, and detailed final speech to make to you. Instead, I feel humbled, quieted, almost silenced.

I can probably squeeze out a few last things about freedom, love, trust, and the core wound.

But I keep feeling we've come into a very holy presence together, where too many more words may get in the way.

So I'll be brief.

You've got the discussions of all these secrets here. You can always return to them and go deeper. You won't exhaust them. You won't make them "un-secrets" by mining their riches ever more deeply.

I've spoken a lot in these considerations about freedom, love, and trust. I'm willing to bet that by now you see how much of those so-desired qualities you get to find when you give yourself permission to feel how little of them you have already found. Make sense?

Like a contrary among the Native Americans, riding his horse backward and making a fool of himself, you give yourself great gifts and spontaneously teach the whole world when you do this mysterious dance of permitting yourself to be as undignified, uncool, and unmasked as these secrets help you remember you really are. Bodily! And *there* is the freedom. *There* is the love. *There* is the trust.

I've introduced you to the core wound. If you've touched it deeply, if you've allowed it to present itself as an essential reality of your life, you will never forget it. And you won't be able to stop becoming increasingly conscious first of it, then in it, then as it.

I'll add a couple of quick, new points just as signals that the road never ends:

First, the core wound is how we register the interface in real life between obvious limits and potential or actual limitlessness. In other words, it is our experience of the juncture between the personal and the impersonal dimensions of our total reality. Therefore, and this is the first new point, the core wound can't properly be equated with only the more personal qualities and history of our wound-patterns, birth traumas, emotional and psychological issues, and the like.

That leads to the second new point: *How* we each register the core wound is unique, but *what* we each register is also somehow the heart of every other human being's reality. At the beginning of this book I spoke of the possibilities of different qualities of great relief for everyday folks heroically living ordinary life, for religious believers, and for spiritual seekers. Each of these kinds of people encounters the core wound in distinctive ways. So does every other possible kind of person. But the singular mystery of it is a mark we all bear. Every single one of us.

So the journey of great relief never ends, for any of us or for All.

And the exploration of the core wound is a gateway into the Mystery where real freedom, real love, and real trust become possible – indeed, inevitable.

In my brief Afterword I offer a few practical suggestions for where you might go from here. It's my hope that never again can the road take you far from your own body's truth, logic, and revelation of secrets. Not in this life, at least.

I pray I've done justice to these sacred secrets our bodies so deeply want and need us to know.

Welcome to the next stage of your journey – and all our journeys, together.

AFTERWORD

"Where Can I Go from Here?"

At the end of *Great Relief* I've tried to indicate that this book itself can take you deeper from now on. Just keep dipping into it. You may very well find that you discover things here as if for the first time, or even literally so – you might not remember even reading them before, though perhaps you know you did!

You can also try the old-reliable approach of opening the book randomly every day, or from time to time, and seeing where your attention lands. (Or doing the same kind of random opening on your cassette or CD.)

As I mentioned earlier, this book has been in the works for several years. For at least the last two years, I had a nagging question about which chapters to add after what eventually became Secret #8, defining the core wound.

Finally the answer to the question came: "As few additional chapters as possible!"

The reason, I saw, is that this book needs essentially to be a self-contained communication. I don't want you, as my reader or listener, to feel like you now have to go jumping off into all kinds of further explorations for your deeper understanding. And that's where additional chapters might have led.

The simple truth is, you don't have to go off into other explorations unless you truly want to. I certainly have other things to offer but this is plenty for now.

My heartfelt recommendation is just to let this whole investigation sink in more fully. Go on about your life and allow these sacred secrets to start percolating through in little and big ways in the midst of all your ordinary concerns and activities. See where they take you!

If you do want to find ways to enhance your appreciation for any or all of what you found here, let me offer three simple recommendations:

1. **Contact my colleagues and me to take our "Great Relief Workshop."** As presently offered, this is a one-day event that literally walks through the secrets of this book and the various exercises. If you have read the book and done all the exercises already, you may feel, "What is a workshop going to give me that I don't already have?" Well, good question; don't attend it if you don't really want more!

   But if you do, the experience of settling deeply into these sacred secrets along with other people in a guided way may well give you a whole other dimension of under-standing and appreciation. Also, the workshops are led by facilitators I've trained, and sometimes by me. We may be able to help you integrate this wisdom in ways that aren't possible on one's own. Here are a couple of comments on the workshop from recent attendees:

   "The Great Relief Workshop was a revelation. It pre-sented me a new way of looking at the human condition using down-to-earth experiences and practical terms that continue to unfold long after the end of the day. It's hard to imagine anyone could take the Great Relief Workshop and not come away with a new understanding of what it means to be a human being. I can't think of many one-day events that have truly changed the course of my inner work. This was one." – *Bill Trout, Richmond, VA*

"The Great Relief Workshop was exquisite, personal, sweet and deep. I felt seen for who I am at the deepest level. I now have an experience of what it means to be human that I can relax into and accept myself from that is quite new for me and welcome. I look forward to deepening the process by doing the exercises in the book." – *Juliette Amoroso, Portland, OR*

We are willing to create and schedule Great Relief Workshops wherever there is sufficient interest, so call us toll-free at 1.888.741.5000 or write to us at greatrelief@earthlink.net to let us know of your interests.

2. **Visit our website, www.wakingdown.org.** Over the last decade I've founded a whole approach to realizing the core wound and living consciously on its basis. The approach is called "Waking Down in Mutuality." I have trained many men and women to help me teach its principles and secrets to those who desire to know more. A visit to our website will show you whether this may be of interest to you.

On the "Events" page of this website you can also find our current schedule of Great Relief Workshops around the United States and in Canada.

3. **Read some of my other books.** The main ones I would recommend now are:

- *Healing the Spirit/Matter Split: An Invitation to Wake Down in Mutuality and Fulfill Your Divinely Human Destiny.* This is a brief (122 pages), conversational introduction to my work and that of my friends and colleagues, just published in early 2004.

- *Waking Down: Beyond Hypermasculine Dharmas – A Breakthrough Way of Self-Realization in the Sanctuary of Mutuality.* This book gives more of a complete overview of the principles and especially early stages of the Waking Down in Mutuality work and transformations. Originally published in 1998.

Also, stay tuned. I mentioned several times in this book that I plan book-length sequels to *Great Relief.* The first will probably be *Great Relief for Frustrated and Unfinished Spiritual Seekers;* the second, *Great Relief for Broken Souls – And for the Broken Zones in Every Body's Psyche.*

But mostly, again, stay tuned to yourself. If the Mystery of being alive prompts you to seek more clarification of the revelations you've found through *Great Relief,* wonderful. If not, that is just fine. I certainly do welcome you to find out more through my other writings or to come to one or more of the events that my friends and/or Linda and I offer. I also welcome the day when I hear from someone that they read this book and have just continued reveling in the great relief that these secrets brought to them two, five, ten, or fifteen years ago.

Keep listening to your body. As in Secret #7, if you're not sure what it really wants, ask it – and then listen for the real answer! One way or another, your body will let you know what it wants and needs. And the real answers will always ultimately be good for others and the world as well as for yourself – even if they include the kind of answer that tells you, for instance, to stop overgiving of yourself and caretaking too much for others just at this time of your life.

Here's the best secret of all: *The more you listen to your body, the more it will reveal its own secrets* – quite apart from anything you can read in books or hear from others.

For me, to know you've made this special discovery would be most gratifying.

After all, I am at liberty to speak or even be aware of only a tiny number of the many secrets your body wants you to know. My job in this book has been to help you make your own body's acquaintance at a new level, where you can freely conduct an unending conversation. As I do, myself.

It's been a great pleasure to share these insights, questions, and mysteries with you, and I wish you the very best.

Saniel Bonder
San Rafael, California

About the Author

Since 1992 Saniel Bonder has helped more than two hundred people fulfill their quests for spiritual enlightenment. A shaman and tantric, he is the author of the classic *Waking Down* and founder of the "Waking Down in Mutuality" teachings. He's also an eco-entrepreneur and an activist for a nuclear-free world, an amateur golfer and flutist, and the devoted husband of his beloved, Linda Groves-Bonder (who sings professionally as Linda Groves).

Saniel's other books include *Healing the Spirit/Matter Split, The Tantra of Trust, The Conscious Principle, Sure Fire,* and a novel, *While Jesus Weeps: Conversations in the Garden of Gethsemane.*